Amun Temples in Nubia

A typological study of New Kingdom, Napatan and Meroitic Temples

Caroline M. Rocheleau

BAR International Series 1850
2008

Published in 2016 by
BAR Publishing, Oxford

BAR International Series 1850

Amun Temples in Nubia

ISBN 978 1 4073 0337 6

© C M Rocheleau and the Publisher 2008

The author's moral rights under the 1988 UK Copyright,
Designs and Patents Act are hereby expressly asserted.

All rights reserved. No part of this work may be copied, reproduced, stored,
sold, distributed, scanned, saved in any form of digital format or transmitted
in any form digitally, without the written permission of the Publisher.

BAR Publishing is the trading name of British Archaeological Reports (Oxford) Ltd.
British Archaeological Reports was first incorporated in 1974 to publish the BAR
Series, International and British. In 1992 Hadrian Books Ltd became part of the BAR
group. This volume was originally published by Archaeopress in conjunction with
British Archaeological Reports (Oxford) Ltd / Hadrian Books Ltd, the Series principal
publisher, in 2008. This present volume is published by BAR Publishing, 2016.

Printed in England

BAR titles are available from:

            BAR Publishing
            122 Banbury Rd, Oxford, OX2 7BP, UK
EMAIL   info@barpublishing.com
PHONE +44 (0)1865 310431
  FAX   +44 (0)1865 316916
            www.barpublishing.com

TABLE OF CONTENTS

ACKNOWLEDGEMENTS v

LIST OF FIGURES vii

LIST OF TABLES ix

CHAPTER 1. INTRODUCTION 1
   INTRODUCTION 1
      Research Goals and Typological Approach 1
      Definition of the Study Corpus 1
      Methodology 2
   REVIEW OF PREVIOUS ACADEMIC RESEARCH 2
   SUMMARY 3

CHAPTER 2. GAZETTEER OF POSTULATED AMUN TEMPLES IN NUBIA 5
   INTRODUCTION 5
   DESCRIPTION OF THE GAZETTEER 5
      Presentation of sites 5
      Site Name, Geographical Location and GPS Coordinates 5
      Fundamental Information 5
      Brief Description and Architectural Plan 6
      Bibliographical References 6
   DESCRIPTION OF REGIONAL DIVISIONS 8
      Lower Nubia 8
      The Batn el-Haggar 8
      The Abri-Delgo Reach 8
      The Dongola Reach 8
      The Abu Hamed Reach 8
      The Bayuda Desert 8
      The Atbara-Khartoum Reach 8
      The Butana 8
      The Gezira 8
   GAZETTEER OF POSTULATED AMUN TEMPLES IN NUBIA 10
      DABOD, Lower Nubia (Egypt) 10
         Chapel of Amun of Dabod 10
      AMADA, Lower Nubia (Egypt) 11
         Temple of Rē-Horakhty (and Amun-Rē?) 11
      ANIBA, Lower Nubia (Egypt) 12
         Postulated Temple of Amun 12
      QASR IBRIM, Lower Nubia (Egypt) 13
         Postulated Temple 13
      GEBEL ADDA, Lower Nubia (Sudan) 14
         Meroitic Temple (dedicated to Amun?) 14
      AKSHA, Lower Nubia (Sudan) 15
         Temple of Amun, Rē, and the deified Ramses II 15
      AMARA EAST, Abri-Delgo Reach (Sudan) 16
         Temple of Amun 16
      AMARA WEST, Abri-Delgo Reach (Sudan) 17
         Temple of Amun-Rē 17
      SAI ISLAND, Abri-Delgo Reach (Sudan) 18
         Temple A 18
      SOLEB, Abri-Delgo Reach (Sudan) 19
         Temple of Amun and Nebmaatrē as his "living image" 19
      SESEBI, Abri-Delgo Reach (Sudan) 20
         Triple Temple of the Theban Triad (?) 20
      DOUKKI GEL, Dongola Reach (Sudan) 21

- *Temple Complex of Amun of Pnubs: West Temple* 21
- *Temple Complex of Amun of Pnubs: West Temple and Annexes* 22
- *Temple Complex of Amun of Pnubs: West and East Temples - Napatan phase* 23
- *Temple Complex of Amun of Pnubs: West and East Temples - Meroitic Phase* 24
- TABO (Argo Island), Dongola Reach (Sudan) 25
  - *Postulated Temple of Amun of Pnubs (?)* 25
- KAWA, Dongola Reach (Sudan) 26
  - *Temple A, Temple of Amun* 26
  - *Temple B, Temple of Amun* 27
  - *Temple T, Temple of Amun of Gematon* 28
- SONIYAT, Dongola Reach (Sudan) 29
  - *Temple TRG40, Napatan phase* 29
  - *Temple TRG40, Meroitic phase* 30
- HUGEIR GUBLI, Dongola Reach (Sudan) 31
  - *Postulated Temple of Amun of Tara-on-ensi* 31
- SANAM ABU DOM, Dongola Reach (Sudan) 32
  - *Temple of Amun, Bull of Nubia* 32
- GEBEL BARKAL, Dongola Reach (Sudan) 33
  - *Temple B500, Great Temple of Amun of Napata* 33
  - *Temple B700, Temple of Amun* 34
  - *Temple of Amun B800-First* 35
  - *Temple of Amun B800-Second* 36
- DANGEIL, Atbara-Khartoum Reach (Sudan) 37
  - *Temple of Amun* 37
- MUTMIR, Atbara-Khartoum Reach (Sudan) 38
  - *Postulated Temple* 38
- MEROE, Atbara-Khartoum Reach (Sudan) 39
  - *Temple KC104* 39
  - *Sun Temple M250* 40
  - *Temple M260, Great Temple of Amun-Nete* 41
  - *Postulated Early Amun Temple (Royal City, Area M292-298)* 42
  - *Isis Temple M600 (previously dedicated to Amun?)* 43
  - *Temple M720* 44
- HAMADAB, Atbara-Khartoum Reach (Sudan) 45
  - *Temple H1000* 45
- AWLIB, Atbara-Khartoum Reach (Sudan) 46
  - *Postulated Temple to Amun* 46
- EL-HASSA, Atbara-Khartoum Reach (Sudan) 47
  - *Temple of Amun of Tabakh* 47
- WAD BAN NAGA, Atbara-Khartoum Reach (Sudan) 48
  - *Temple WBN300* 48
  - *Temple WBN500* 49
- ALEM, Butana (Sudan) 50
  - *Meroitic Temple* 50
- DUANIB, Butana (Sudan) 51
  - *Temple I, Postulated Temple to Amun* 51
- MUSAWWARAT ES-SUFRA, Butana (Sudan) 52
  - *Temple IA 100* 52
- UMM SODA, Butana (Sudan) 53
  - *Postulated Temple* 53
- NAGA, Butana (Sudan) 54
  - *Temple N100, Temple of Amun of Tolkte* 54
  - *Temple N500, Temple of Amun* 55
- SOBA EAST, Gezira (Sudan) 56
  - *Postulated Temple* 56

CHAPTER 3. IDENTIFICATION OF AMUN TEMPLES IN NUBIA 57

INTRODUCTION 57
THE DIFFICULTIES OF IDENTIFICATION 57

- IDENTIFICATION OF AMUN TEMPLES 59
  - *Temples Identified by Inscriptions and Rams* 59
  - *Temples Identified by an Inscription* 59
  - *Temples Identified by Ram Statues* 60
  - *Ram God without a Temple* 60
- IDENTIFICATION OF ANCIENT PNUBS 61
- INCONCLUSIVE IDENTIFICATION OF TEMPLE OR SITE 62
- SUMMARY 66

CHAPTER 4. TYPOLOGY OF AMUN TEMPLES IN NUBIA 68

- INTRODUCTION 68
- TYPOLOGY OF AMUN TEMPLES 68
- GROUP A: SINGLE-ROOM TEMPLES 68
  - *Group A, Regular Type* 68
- GROUP B: MULTI-ROOM TEMPLES 68
- MULTI-ROOM WITH BASIC PLAN 69
  - *Group B.1: Regular Type* 69
- MULTI-ROOM WITH COMPLEX PLAN 69
  - *Group B.2: Regular Type* 70
  - *Group B.2: Jubilee Type* 70
  - *Group B.2: Coronation Type* 70
  - *Group B.2: Amanitore Type* 71
- ADDITIONAL CLASSIFICATION EXERCISE 72
- SUMMARY 72

CHAPTER 5. SOME REMAINING ISSUES 76

- UNRESOLVED ISSUES AT PNUBS 76
  - *The Coronation Temple of Pnubs* 76
  - *Tabo or not Tabo?* 76
- ARCHITECTURE & CULT PRACTICES 77
  - *The So-Called Dais Room* 77
  - *The Ramps and Platform at Naga* 78
  - *Single Sanctuary versus Triple Sanctuary* 79
- THE QUESTION OF MEROE 79
  - *Garstang and the Great Temple of Amun* 79
  - *The Issue of the Early Napatan Temple* 80
- SUMMARY 81

CHAPTER 6. ANALYSIS, INTERPRETATION, AND CONCLUSION 82

- ANALYSIS AND INTERPRETATION 82
- CONCLUDING REMARKS 83

ABBREVIATIONS 86

REFERENCE LIST 86

INDEX 94

ACKNOWLEDGEMENTS

The research on which this book is based was undertaken for the degree of Doctor of Philosophy at the University of Toronto, Toronto, Canada (2005). After a successful dissertation defence, Drs Krzysztof A. Grzymski, doctoral thesis advisor, and William Y. Adams, external examiner, urged me to publish the results of the research for its relevance to current Nubian studies. For their unwavering support and encouragement, I am most grateful.

Since 2005, I have revised the typology and incorporated materials unavailable at the time of writing together with recent archaeological data relevant to the research project. Thanks must go to Dr Julie R. Anderson, The British Museum, for her keen Nubiological eye in editing the final manuscript as well as my colleagues at the North Carolina Museum of Art and the Department of Cultural Resources for their additional editorial advice, John W. Coffey, Tiara L. Paris and Jennifer French, and their technical support, Natalia J. Lonchyna and Karen C. Kelly.

LIST OF FIGURES

Figure 1: Map of Nubia, Physiographic Divisions 7
Figure 2: Map of Nubia, Amun Temple Sites 9
Figure 3: Dabod, Chapel of Amun 10
Figure 4: Amada, Temple of Rē-Horakhty (and Amun-Rē?) 11
Figure 5: Gebel Adda, Meroitic Temple 14
Figure 6: Aksha, Temple of Amun, Rē, and the deified Ramses II 15
Figure 7: Amara East, Temple of Amun 16
Figure 8: Amara West, Temple of Amun-Rē 17
Figure 9: Sai Island, Temple A 18
Figure 10: Soleb, Temple of Amun and Nebmaatrē 19
Figure 11: Sesebi, Triple Temple of the Theban Triad (?) 20
Figure 12: Doukki Gel, Temple Complex of Amun of Pnubs, West Temple 21
Figure 13: Doukki Gel, Temple Complex of Amun of Pnubs, West Temple and Annexes 22
Figure 14: Doukki Gel, Temple Complex of Amun of Pnubs, West and East Temples (Napatan) 23
Figure 15: Doukki Gel, Temple Complex of Amun of Pnubs, West and East Temples (Meroitic) 24
Figure 16: Tabo, Postulated Temple of Amun of Pnubs (?) 25
Figure 17: Kawa, Temple A 26
Figure 18: Kawa, Temple B 27
Figure 19: Kawa, Temple T 28
Figure 20: Soniyat, Temple TRG40, Napatan phase 29
Figure 21: Soniyat, Temple TRG40, Meroitic phase 30
Figure 22: Hugeir Gubli, Postulated Temple of Amun of Tara-on-ensi 31
Figure 23: Sanam Abu Dom, Temple of Amun, Bull of Nubia 32
Figure 24: Gebel Barkal, Temple B500 33
Figure 25: Gebel Barkal, Temple B700 34
Figure 26: Gebel Barkal, Temple B800-First 35
Figure 27: Gebel Barkal, Temple B800-Second 36
Figure 28: Dangeil, Temple of Amun 37
Figure 29: Meroe, Temple KC104 39
Figure 30: Meroe, Sun Temple M250 40
Figure 31: Meroe, Temple M260 41
Figure 32: Meroe, Postulated Early Amun Temple in Royal City M292-298 42
Figure 33: Meroe, Isis Temple M600 43
Figure 34: Meroe, Temple M720 44
Figure 35: Hamadab, Temple H1000 45
Figure 36: Awlib, Postulated Temple of Amun 46
Figure 37: Wad ban Naga, Temple WBN300 48
Figure 38: Wad ban Naga, Temple WBN500 49
Figure 39: Alem, Meroitic Temple 50
Figure 40: Musawwarat es-Sufra, Temple IA 100 52
Figure 41: Naga, Temple N100 54
Figure 42: Naga, Temple N500 55

LIST OF TABLES

Table 1: Identification of Amun Temples 67
Table 2: Typology of Amun Temples 74
Table 3: Additional Typological Exercise 75

CHAPTER 1. INTRODUCTION

INTRODUCTION

Whether in Egypt or in Nubia, the god Amun played the most important role in the legitimisation of kingship, and thus Amun was not only the *king of the gods* (*nsw ntrw*), he was also the god favoured by the kings. Kings were chosen by the will of Amun to become the next ruler and thus had a legitimate claim to the throne. In return, rulers thanked their divine father with lavish rituals and demonstrated their piety by commissioning temples in his honour. As a result, from the Eighteenth Dynasty onwards, approximately fifty temples dedicated (or thought to be) to Amun were constructed in Nubia alone.

As new architectural data surface with each excavation season, the need for a new comparative study of temples arises. In the current work, previous temple typologies and the most recent information pertaining to Amun temples in Nubia have been combined to create the most up-to-date formal typology and exhaustive gazetteer of Amun temples in Nubia.

Research Goals and Typological Approach
The aims of the study were, first of all, to observe patterns in the spatial configuration of Egyptian and Kushite temples dedicated to Amun in Nubia; second, to identify architectural models; and finally, to ascribe these models to certain historical periods or specific rulers.

A comparative typological approach was judged best to understand spatial configuration and illustrate architectural models because the temples would be regrouped according to common features. A frequent purpose of classification is to permit the formal comparison of materials from different sites, areas or different periods (Adams and Adams 1991: 159). Typological studies are prevalent in archaeology and can apply to assemblages of all shapes and sizes, including temples. In the past, this type of study has yielded important information and made significant contributions to the fields of Egyptology and Nubiology (Török 1984a: 351). The monumental work of A. Badawy on ancient Egyptian architecture (1954, 1960, 1966, and 1968), the numerous publications on tombs, pyramids, and temples by D. Arnold (notably 1971, 1987, 1992, and 1999) as well as the respective typologies of Kushite architecture by W.Y. Adams (1984), A. M. A. Hakem (1988), and S. Wenig (1984) are the most noteworthy of such studies.

Certain scholars, however, find the method of comparison doubtful and prefer a more scientific approach, such as metrology, in order to understand the underlying architectural principles established by ancient architects (Hinkel 1991: 221). Metrological studies focus on units of measurement, harmonic proportion systems, and principles of architectural design that express intrinsic values of a given society and/or historical period via architectural remains (Hinkel 1991: 220). Although the latter approach can provide interesting results, the fact remains that the studied buildings were constructed two to three thousand years ago and most are in extremely deteriorated state. Metrological studies based on the measurements obtained from collapsed or reconstructed buildings are by no means accurate (Welsby: personal communication). Seismic activity, floods and subsequent water erosion, heavy vehicular and pedestrian traffic, and *sebakhin* activity all have disastrous effects on the precarious stability of ancient masonry. The dislocation of stone blocks and bricks as well as the overall destruction of the monument greatly affect this attempt to attain the greatest precision and exactness. Moreover, the appearance of maximum precision and accuracy holds a rather illusory quality (Schiff-Giorgini *et al.* 2002: 8). Ancient Egyptian and Kushite temples were not perfect, certainly not when it came to measurements. As Lepsius expressed, "[…] verifying measures of the most splendid buildings dated to the height of that civilisation has demonstrated that seldom is a side of a building exactly of the same length as the opposite, that in majestic colonnades the intervals between columns vary, that they were not strict with right angles in courtyards […]" (St-John 2001: 4-5).[1] In spite of these technical imperfections, the plan remains most important because the distribution of rooms suggests that the architects thought of the cult practices and ceremonies to be performed in the temple as part of the architectural planning process (Ricke 1944: 3ff; Heitzmann 1976: 10-11; Kemp 1989: 97). The famous dictum "form follows function"[2] is the underlying architectural principle found in the present architectural study. Ricke and Schott have hypothesised that the same principle applies to ancient Egyptian architecture. Ricke states that the structure of edifices—whether it is a massive burial mound or a series of courtyards—is in essence identical because the architectural layout is defined by building methods and skill, as well as (and more importantly) driven by practical needs and function (1944: 11).[3] In such light, it is not difficult to accept that a typological study will provide as reliable results and observations as any other study.

Definition of the Study Corpus
Pious kings and megalomaniac pharaohs spent great fortunes in erecting superb architectural monuments in

---

[1] Translation of Lepsius' *Die Altägyptische Elle und Ihre Eintheilung*, Berlin, Königlichen Akademie der Wissenschaften, 1865.
[2] The actual phrase "form follows function" was coined by American architect, Louis Henry Sullivan (1856-1924), who is known as the "father of functionalism." It appears in Sullivan's 1896 article "The Tall Office Building Artistically Considered" published in *Lippincotfs* 57.
[3] Studies of architectural plans and layouts of architectural complexes can be extremely insightful and can illustrate not only the function of a building, but also, for example, the social structure/hierarchy of a particular civilisation. The works of Macy Roth on Old Kingdom funerary complexes (1993) can be noted as such an example.

honour of their divine father, Amun. Each of these monuments, in order to be included in the typology, must possess the defining features of the typology itself. In the present typology, the contextual invariants[4] are clearly defined in space (geographical territory) and time (historical periods), and the intrinsic feature is clearly identified (free-standing temple). These definitions are of utmost importance, particularly because the contextual features of space and time are interrelated.

Contextual Invariant No.1: Geographical Territory
Nubia is, needless to say, an extensive study area; yet, it could not be reduced geographically without creating a biased study sample. As specific regions of Nubia are associated with specific historical periods, regions picked at random would skew results. Within the historical timeframe of the study, the north of Nubia is predominantly New Kingdom Egyptian with a large concentration of Napatan sites between the Third and Fourth Cataracts, while the south is almost exclusively Meroitic. Therefore, for the purpose of this study, Nubia is defined as the territory that extends from the First Cataract to a little south of Khartoum.

Contextual Invariant No. 2: Historical Periods
Ancient Egypt played such a significant role in the development of monumental architecture in Nubia that the inclusion of New Kingdom temples within the defined geographical area was deemed essential. Indigenous religious architectural tradition in Nubia evolved in a rather erratic fashion, if evolution is a concept that can be used to describe the few architectural attempts at constructing cult temples and funerary chapels prior to the Twenty-fifth Dynasty. The current archaeological record leads one to believe that temples were not intrinsic to local Nubian cultures and traditions, but were the result of direct contacts with Egypt. Therefore, the historical periods under consideration are the Egyptian New Kingdom (c. 1540—1075 BCE) and the Kushite period, divided into its two phases, the Napatan (including the Twenty-fifth Dynasty) (c. 1000—310 BCE) and the Meroitic (c. 275 BCE—350 CE) periods. In charts and legends, these periods are abbreviated to NK, Dyn. 25, NP, and MK respectively.

Definition of the Intrinsic Feature: Temple
New Kingdom pharaohs commonly used three forms of temple structures: the *speos*, the *hemispeos*, and the free-standing temple (Tsinoyeva 1993: 399, 403-404). However, a brief review of Kushite architecture revealed the existence of extremely few rock-cut or semi-rock-cut temples. Only two examples are known for the Napatan period: temples B200 (dedicated to Hathor, Tefnut, and an unknown goddess) and B300 (dedicated to the goddess Mut), both hewn inside the Holy Mountain at Gebel Barkal by Taharqo (Hakem 1988: 142; Kendall 1992a: 140). A small Meroitic rock shrine dedicated to the criocephalic Amun existed at Gebel Qeili (Hofmann and Tomandl 1986: 121ff; Zach and Tomandl 2000: 144). Considering the paucity of comparative material dated to the Napatan and Meroitic periods, the obvious decision was taken: the study corpus would be restricted to the predominant type of temple architecture common to the entire region and the three historical periods—the free-standing temple.

The above invariants can be summed up in a few words: "Nubian," "New Kingdom/Napatan/Meroitic," and "free-standing temple" and the study corpus is thus clearly defined.

Methodology
Although the author's archaeological work and visit to various temple sites in Nubia[5] greatly facilitated the research aspect of the project, the bulk of it, however, remained the comparative study of the published architectural plans of the temples in the corpus. Ultimately, with the exception of the Amun Temple of el-Hassa,[6] it was possible to obtain the plans for all the positively identified Amun temples. Amongst the inconclusively identified buildings, it was impossible to find an actual plan of the various structures and *kôms* at Duanib.

The typological methodology is explained in its context in Chapter 4, but a few preliminary words are necessary. As the research project concentrated solely on temple architecture, its focus was the spatial configuration of the temples possibly identified as Amun temples. How many rooms are there? Where are they located and how do they connect? Are there special rooms or features that distinguish certain temples? Thus, the numerous temples were organised in groups and sub-groups. The thought process behind the elaboration of this classification scheme was primarily deductive, creating categories based on general attributes and sub-dividing according to details and finer characteristics.

REVIEW OF PREVIOUS ACADEMIC RESEARCH

Two typological studies of Kushite (Napatan and Meroitic) architecture were presented approximately

---

[4] The terminology adopted for the present work follows that of Adams W.Y. and E.W. Adams in *Archaeological Typology and Practical Reality: A Dialectical Approach to Artifact Classification and Sorting*. Cambridge: Cambridge University Press, 1991.

[5] The author participated in the excavation work of the Canadian-Sudanese Meroe Expedition (2000-2004) and the Berber-Abidiya Archaeological Project (2002-03; 2006-07) and wishes to thank the project directors for their support: Drs Krzysztof Grzymski, Ali Osman, Julie Anderson, and Salah Mohamed Ahmed. Additional thanks must go to colleagues who allowed or arranged visits to their temple sites: Kerma/Doukki Gel, Soniyat, Hugeir Gubli, Gebel Barkal, Awlib, el-Hassa, Musawwarat es-Sufra, and Naga. They know who they are.

[6] Although the excavation work of the Amun Temple at el-Hassa is completed, the complex stratigraphy and architectural sequencing were, as of December 2007, still under study (Vincent Rondot, personal communication). The plan of the temple remains unpublished and unavailable for study.

twenty years ago, that of A. M. A. Hakem (1988) and S. Wenig (1984). W.Y. Adams also studied Kushite architecture and presented the results of his research at the Meroitic Conference in 1980 (published in 1984). In recent years, P. Wolf has been working on temples of the "Meroitic South," focussing solely on buildings of that period located in the Island of Meroe (2006). Although not considered architectural or typological studies, the work of M. Zach and H. Tomandl (2000) on the identification of Meroitic Amun temples and shrines across Nubia as well as the recent publication by I. Guermeur on the cults of Amun outside of Thebes (2005) must still be noted.

Unlike the present research, the previous studies focussed on general religious architecture and grouped buildings into functionally-defined types such as temples, pyramid chapels, and kiosks. They can therefore be considered a stepping stone for this research project, which focuses only on one architectural type (the free-standing temple) dedicated to one god (but allowing for guest cults). As a stimulus for the current research, these early typologies must be briefly examined.

Hakem's typology distinguished two groups of temples, "Amun Temples" and "Lion Temples," a basic two-fold division that met with criticism. The first category was defined as large temples with the ubiquitous Egyptian plan—pylon gateway, forecourt, hypostyle hall, pronaos and naos, with adjoining auxiliary rooms; while the second category was comprised of buildings associated with the cult of the Meroitic lion god, Apedemak. According to Adams, Hakem was unquestionably correct in recognising the distinguishing characteristics of the elaborate axial structure of the Egyptian-type temples (mostly Napatan) and much simpler Meroitic buildings consisting of one or two rooms (1984: 258). However, Adams as well as Bradley (1984b: 281) and Wenig (1984: 383ff) pointed out the obvious problem with the nomenclature of the types. First, the division was "over simplified" (Adams 1984: 258); not all the temples of the Amun Temple category were dedicated to Amun, nor were all those in the Lion Temple category related to the cult of Apedemak. Second, the fact that a temple was a multi-room temple did not exclusively indicate that this building was dedicated to Amun. As Wenig's study has demonstrated, multi-room temples were most often dedicated to Egyptian deities, a number of which other than Amun were venerated in Nubia—notably Isis, Hathor, and Horus. Therefore a temple—large or small—that followed the basic Egyptian temple plan was not necessarily dedicated to Amun, unless there was an inscription confirming this cultic dedication or there were rams associated with this building (see the selection criteria mentioned in Chapter 3). Wenig's typology remedied this problem by dividing his temples into *Mehrraumtempel* and *Einraumtempel* categories (multi-room and single-room temples, respectively). This visually expressive and architecturally-based nomenclature was adopted for the current study.

Although Wenig's work has been a valuable contribution to the field, it had certain pitfalls, which have already been pointed out by Wolf (2006: 240). The expressed idea that only Egyptian deities could be worshipped in multi-room temples makes impossible the syncretism between Amun and a Meroitic deity, or the possibility of the guest cult of a local god within a multi-room Amun temple. Our modern monotheistic view of religious structures skews our perception of the Egyptian temple, and by extension the Kushite temple, where the possibility of multiple cults in a single building existed (Heitzmann 1976: 9-10). It also implied that Amun could not be worshipped in smaller one-room or two-room temples. Indeed, the classifications proposed by Wenig and Hakem made a distinction based on the cultural origin of the deity (Egyptian or Kushite) and only Egyptian deities were worshipped in multi-room temples, while local deities were associated with single-room temples.

SUMMARY

Essentially, the author's doctoral dissertation was a typological study based on the comparison of architectural plans of one type of building dedicated to a particular deity. The study corpus was restricted to a very specific region (albeit quite extensive) and it spanned several centuries that could be divided into three distinct historical periods. Although it used two earlier typological studies of Kushite architecture as a stepping stone, this study differed in the definition of its assemblage. Compared to Hakem and Wenig's general classifications, the current corpus was restricted to one functional type, which was itself focussed on a single architectural type, and the identity of one deity.

The main and most noticeable difference between this research project and the above mentioned typological studies is the fact that the present corpus includes New Kingdom temples in an attempt to follow the architectural evolution of Kushite temples from their source of inspiration. Because ancient Egyptian temples were undoubtedly the prototypes upon which Napatan and Meroitic temples were modelled, it was necessary to include them in the study and classify them together with later temples in order to properly establish patterns.

Additionally, the newly uncovered temples at Doukki Gel, Hugeir Gubli, Usli, Soniyat, Dangeil, and el-Hassa offered new material that needed to be included in such a study. The opportunity to incorporate the latest discoveries into one's research could not be passed up. As much as the study of Egyptian temples contributed to our understanding of ancient Egyptian civilisation, the study of Napatan and Meroitic temples might just do the same for the Kushite kingdom.

CHAPTER 2. GAZETTEER OF POSTULATED AMUN TEMPLES IN NUBIA

Introduction

A thorough architectural study of Amun temples located in Nubian territory necessitates the compilation of a list including all the structures positively identified as temples dedicated to Amun as well as all other temples that scholars believe, in some way, could potentially be a sacred building in honour of this god. The format best suited for the display of such data is that of a gazetteer. However, within the present study, the concept of the gazetteer has been expanded beyond a mere listing of place names to include pertinent historical and archaeological information, an architectural description, an architectural plan, and relevant references.

Description of the Gazetteer

Presentation of sites
As mentioned above, and in keeping with its function, the gazetteer provides a list of (postulated) Amun temple sites across Nubia. The listing of sites within such an extensive territory—the whole of Egyptian and Sudanese Nubia—necessitates a logical structure for its display. Using the works of Adams (1977), Edwards (1989), and Hein (1991) as models, the geographical approach was deemed the most appropriate for the presentation of the temple sites. Thus, all Amun temple sites have been catalogued from north to south, starting at the First Cataract and ending past the Sixth Cataract, slightly south of Khartoum, at Soba East. The physiographic division of the territory is based on that suggested by Adams (1977) and Edwards (1989), and comprises the following regions: Lower Nubia, the Batn el-Haggar, the Abri-Delgo Reach, the Dongola Reach, the Abu Hamed Reach, the Bayuda Desert, the Khartoum-Atbara Reach, the Butana, and the Gezira (see Figure 1).

The adoption of the north-to-south (upstream) reading of the map of Nubia is not only logical, it is further justified by the evolution of temple architecture in Nubia, which was greatly influenced by historical events such as the ever-growing New Kingdom expansion into Nubia, the rise of the Napatan Empire/Twenty-Fifth Dynasty as well as the Kushites' eventual move south to the Meroitic heartland.

Site Name, Geographical Location and GPS Coordinates
Within each region, the sites are listed following the winding course of the Nile as one would come across them sailing upstream (see Figure 2). Confusion caused by the location of a site on the east or west bank at the various bends of the river has been avoided by simply indicating the location on the right or left bank, as one would locate them when reading a map. However, "east" and "west" have been retained for localities that includes a district on each bank, as is the case with Amara East and Amara West.

Additionally, with the single exception of Gebel Adda, all cardinal points mentioned within this dissertation are all true compass points, not "local directions" based on the course of the Nile River as favoured by late nineteenth century explorers and early twentieth century archaeologists.

Certain archaeological sites have been identified by more than one appellation over the years, further complicating site identification. Additional names, identified during the course of the research, are included in [square brackets] for the purpose of clarification. However, variant spellings of place names are not included.

Each site is further identified by its Global Positioning System (GPS) coordinates in degrees (D), minutes (M), and, whenever relevant, seconds (S). Although most GPS software and databases process the coordinates in degrees, decimal minutes (.m), and decimal seconds (.s), atlases and maps continue the use of the regular DMS system. Thus, all information has been converted to this more widely understood system whenever necessary. GPS information for New Kingdom and Napatan Amun temple sites is taken from the Baines and Málek *Atlas of Ancient Egypt* (1980). In the case of Meroitic sites, which are not listed in Baines and Málek, the GPS coordinates were taken from Hintze's Butana Expedition report (1959) or kindly provided by the current site excavators.

Fundamental Information
Occasionally, the sites listed are home to more than one temple dedicated to Amun and fundamental information is necessary in order to properly identify each temple. Consequently, the name of the temple, its numerical or alphabetical identification, and its location on a specific *kôm* are included. This information is particularly useful when trying to correlate information obtained from much earlier excavation and survey reports. Note that the alphanumerical temple ID or site name is used to designate and refer to temples from this chapter onwards, as is commonly done in Nubian and Meroitic studies.

More historical and archaeological information such as the historical period and the names of the monarchs who commissioned the construction or repairs was deemed important as it helps to establish patterns and models as well as pinpoint specific architectural features to a specific historical period or the reign of a particular ruler. More technical data, such as the orientation of the building (the first cardinal point being the entrance), the construction materials, and the preservation status of the temple, are also included.

Despite the fact that a metrological approach was considered futile to study a corpus of ruinous buildings, measurements of the overall temple are nonetheless included if only to provide a mental picture of the size of the building. Measurements are provided in metres (m), the modern unit used by archaeologists in excavation reports. Also included in [square brackets] next to the modern measurement is the ancient unit of measure applicable to the particular temple. Egyptian architects of the New Kingdom used the royal cubit [c], which is approximately 52.3 to 52.5 cm, and used the inner harmonic proportion system (Hinkel 1991: 220). However, Meroitic architects, greatly influenced by the Hellenes, preferred using the Greek module [M] and the outer harmonic proportion system for their own typical buildings, all the while using the Egyptian royal cubit for Egyptianising monuments (Hinkel 1991: 221). Unlike the Egyptian cubit, or our own modern metre for that matter, the module is not a fixed unit of measure *per se*. The module is the base unit (different for each building) with which the proportion system functions. This base unit is generally equal to the lower diameter of a column or, if there are no columns present, the thickness of a wall. The measurement is then multiplied by the most perfect number (number 16) to obtain the width of the pylon, from which the rest of the proportions can be calculated (Hinkel 1987: 152; 1991: 222). However, the Meroites do not appear to have been always consistent. Several modules can be used in the architectural planning of a single building or, occasionally, they will use the Egyptian cubit in a typical Meroitic structure, for example temple M250 at Meroe.

The published description of the architectural layout of a temple is, however, too often inadequate, frustratingly lacking in important details that were overlooked or considered insignificant by early excavators, thus leaving the next generation of scholars without valuable archaeological information. Sometimes, especially in old site reports, measurements of a temple are simply not included or the information does not provide anything beyond the inclusion of a scale on a plan. In such cases, the drawn scale itself had to be used to measure the plan and obtain approximate measurements to provide a mental picture of the size of the building. An asterisk (*) identifies these measurements. In the event that a temple has not survived well the passage of time or has been only partly excavated, the approximate or incomplete measurements are indicated by " ~ " or "(incomplete)," respectively.

Brief Description and Architectural Plan
With the plans of the Amun temples across Nubia being the core of the architectural comparison of the present research thesis, the inclusion of the plan of each discovered and excavated temple is absolutely essential. Although the relevant temple plan is included with each gazetteer entry, a brief description of the various parts of the temple—rams, kiosks, pylons, courts, annex rooms, and other relevant features—is included to provide the reader with architectural vocabulary used in later chapters. Each feature is presented in the order one would reach it if walking along the processional avenue towards the temple, through the courts, and into the sanctuary. The measurements mentioned in the Fundamental Information section are also included on the plan. However it was not possible to insert a scale for many of these plans because several were selected and enlarged from site maps or the original publication did not even include a scale. The inclusion of the measurements should suffice to give an idea of the size of the building.

With the exception of M260 at Meroe, all temple plans were digitised by the author and adapted to follow a common format. The author's plan of the temple at Dangeil has become the Mission's official plan and has been modified slightly since. On these plans, the construction materials are clearly identified: black equals sandstone; dark grey (lines), red brick; and light grey (dots), mud brick. In cases where these materials are not identified on the original published plan, the walls are simply outlined. Solid grey walls refer to the building into which the temple was integrated (see for example Dabod, below). These buildings are not part of the study.

Bibliographical References
The information presented in the Gazetteer was gathered from numerous publications; these are listed in alphabetical order in the Select Bibliographical References section instead of footnotes or notes inserted in the text itself. Each reference is abbreviated to the basic author-date format, but the full reference information is available in the Reference List.

Figure 1: Map of Nubia, Physiographic Divisions

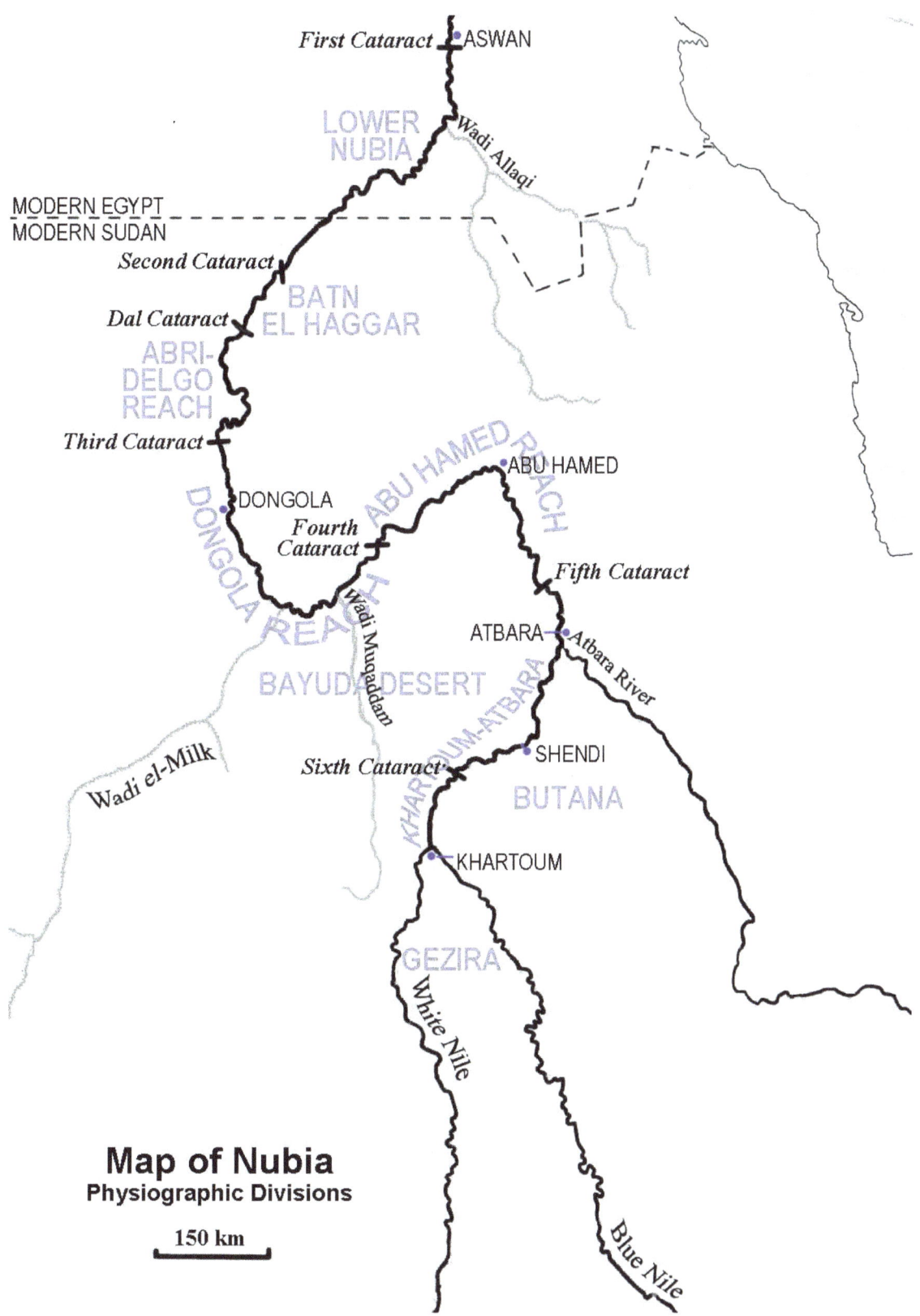

DESCRIPTION OF REGIONAL DIVISIONS

Lower Nubia
Lower Nubia is the only region that falls within the modern boundaries of the Arab Republic of Egypt. It consists of the territory extending from the First to the Second Cataract, which is almost completely under Lake Nasser at the present time. Fortunately, several temples were rescued from the rising waters of the reservoir lake, dismantled, and relocated on higher grounds or re-assembled in museums or parks across the world.

The Batn el-Haggar
The Batn el-Haggar, the most barren and uninhabitable of all regions, is located between the Second and the Dal cataracts, in the northernmost province of Sudan. This desolate region did not attract many Egyptian colonists and Kushite settlers, and there have been no Amun temples located in this part of Nubia.

The Abri-Delgo Reach
The Abri-Delgo Reach refers to the riverine region that stretches south of the Dal Cataract to the Third Cataract. Architectural remains attest to New Kingdom expansion past the Batn el-Haggar.

The Dongola Reach
The Dongola Reach stretches from the Third to the Fourth Cataract. The great ed-Debba bend divides this extensive and important archaeological region in two sections, the northern and the southern Dongola Reach. Within the present study, no distinction will be made between the north and the south.

The Abu Hamed Reach
The Abu Hamed Reach extends from the Fourth Cataract to the Fifth Cataract. Until very recently, no archaeological excavations had been undertaken in this remote region of Nubia. As Edwards mentions (1989: 81; Edwards and el-Amin 2000: 44), the only archaeological activity in the area consisted of regional reconnaissance surveys. Coupled with early travellers' journals and reports, these surveys remained the main source of knowledge of this region until now. Although Adams said the region was "devoid of important remains from Napatan-Meroitic civilization" (1977: 31-2), the lack of proper archaeological investigation may be the reason for this blank archaeological record. The Merowe-Hamdab Dam Project has forced archaeologists into action; several salvage archaeology projects and surveys have been undertaken in the Abu Hamed Reach (el-Tayeb 1998: 35; Mohammed and Hussein 1999: 60), and numerous reports have been published (notably Welsby 2003) or presented at conferences. At the time of writing, there had been no identification of temples dating to the New Kingdom or Napatan and Meroitic periods in the region.

The Bayuda Desert
The Bayuda Desert is the arid area circumscribed by the S-bend of the Nile in the east and Wadi el-Milk in the west. The area is generally described as *terra incognita* because very little archaeological activity has been undertaken in the region. However, our knowledge of the desert has greatly increased in the past few years because the construction of the paved road from Omdurman to ed-Debba necessitated survey of the proposed route and its vicinity. The Sudan Archaeological Research Society (SARS) has reported numerous sites of various periods along the path of construction (Mallinson 1996). Sites have also been noticed (quite often by sheer luck) by archaeologists travelling off the desert motor track on their way to or from Khartoum. In 1996, T. Kendall and his crew reported the discovery of an unexpected Meroitic site—al-Meragh—near the Wadi Muqaddam, between Korti and Tamtam (2000: 1). This site has been ascribed to the Meroitic period based on surface finds, scattered sandstone column drums, and partial excavations. The excavators believe that what appears to be a Meroitic town with several luxurious residences would very likely include temples, although none have been found to date (Kendall 2000: 9). The results of future excavations are much anticipated.

The Atbara-Khartoum Reach
The Atbara-Khartoum Reach, also known as the Shendi Reach (Adams 1977), is the riverine region extending from the Atbara River to the confluence of the Blue and White Niles at Khartoum. This zone, together with the Butana, is known as the Meroitic heartland.

The Butana
The Butana, which is often called the "Island of Meroe," is the region circumscribed by the Atbara, the Blue Nile, and the road from Khartoum to Kassala (Hintze 1959: 171). Much confusion arises because the Butana is divided in four smaller territories based on environment, water, vegetation, and soil distribution, one of which is also called "Butana" (Edwards 1989: 30). Following the example of Hintze (1959), for the sake of simplicity within this study, the Butana refers only to the semi-arid steppeland where Amun temples have been located.

The Gezira
The Gezira is defined as the region comprising both the riverine sectors along the White and the Blue Niles and the hinterland between the two rivers (Edwards 1989: 40). Very little archaeological activity has been undertaken in this part of Sudan and therefore the presence of Amun temples is only postulated.

Figure 2: Map of Nubia, Amun Temple Sites

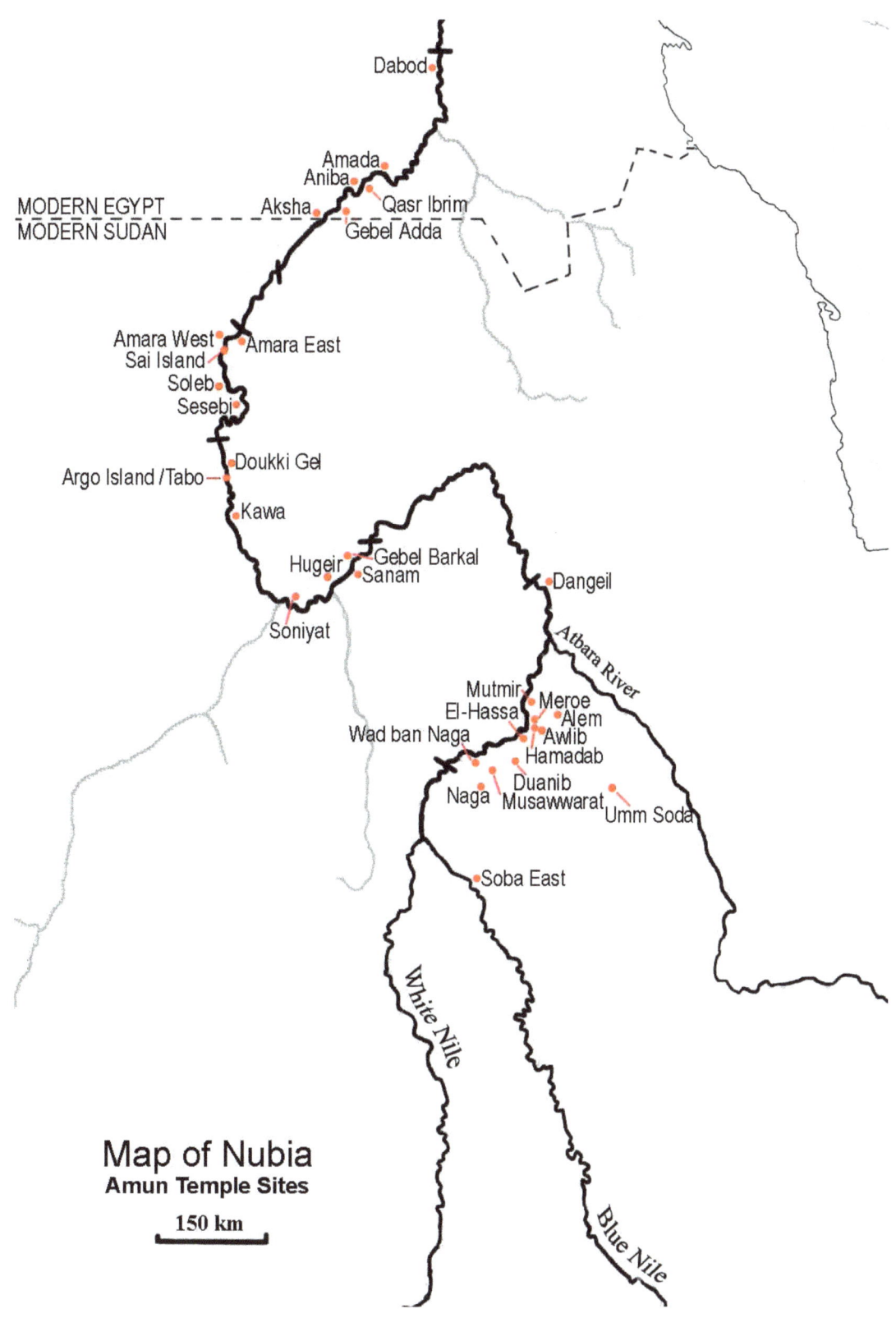

GAZETTEER OF POSTULATED AMUN TEMPLES IN NUBIA

DABOD, Lower Nubia (Egypt)
GPS (DMS): 23.55N 32.52E / Left bank (now in Madrid)

Chapel of Amun of Dabod

Period: Meroitic
Builder(s): Adikhalamani
Orientation: East-west
Measurements: 7 x 5 metres [N/A]
Construction materials: Sandstone
Preservation status: Full height, almost intact.

Brief Architectural Description:
The small chapel at Dabod was a single-room building later incorporated into a Ptolemaic temple dedicated to Amun of Dabod and Isis of the Abaton.

Select Bibliographical References:
Arnold 1992: 90; 2003: 64; Baines and Málek 1980: 180; Clère 1977: 107-113; Gau 1822-1827: pl. 2-6; Guermeur 2005: 477ff; Hein 1991: 5; LÄ I: 997-998; Murray 1931: 189-191; PM VII: 4; Roeder 1911-1912.

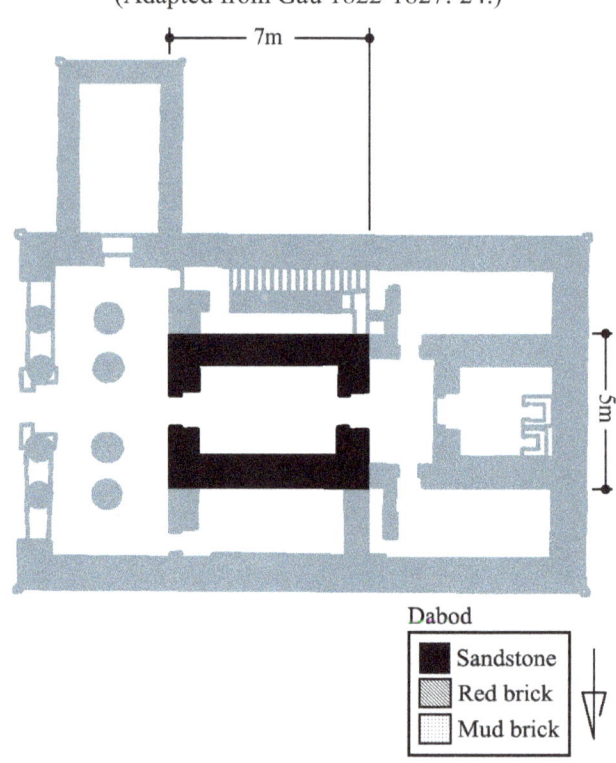

Figure 3: Dabod, Chapel of Amun (Adapted from Gau 1822-1827: 24.)

AMADA, Lower Nubia (Egypt)
GPS (DMS): 22.43N 32.15E / Right bank
[Hassaia]

Temple of Rē-Horakhty (and Amun-Rē?)

Period:	New Kingdom, Dyn. 18 and 19
Builder(s):	Thutmosis III / Amenhotep II (core); Thutmosis IV (hypostyle); Seti I / Ramses II (repairs)
Orientation:	West-east, facing the Nile River
Measurements:	23.60 x 9.75 metres [c]
Construction materials:	Sandstone, brick
Preservation status:	Over 4 metres high in some areas, preserved lintels.

Brief Architectural Description:
The entrance of this small temple is a portal/pylon that leads into a hypostyle hall that had originally been a simple portico. The next room is a transverse vestibule that opens into three sanctuaries that are linked together by small chambers (on the sides) and the back of the main sanctuary.

Select Bibliographical References:
el-Achiery, Barguet, and Dewachter 1967; Arnold 1992: 82; Badawy 1968: 273; Barguet and Dewachter 1967; Barguet *et al.* 1967; Dewachter 1987: 190-193; Gauthier 1913-1926; Gohany 1998: 54-58; Guermeur 2005: 490-491; Hein 1991: 20-23; Murray 1931: 222-224; PM VII: 65-73.

Figure 4: Amada, Temple of Rē-Horakhty (and Amun-Rē?)
(Adapted from Hein 1991: 188.)

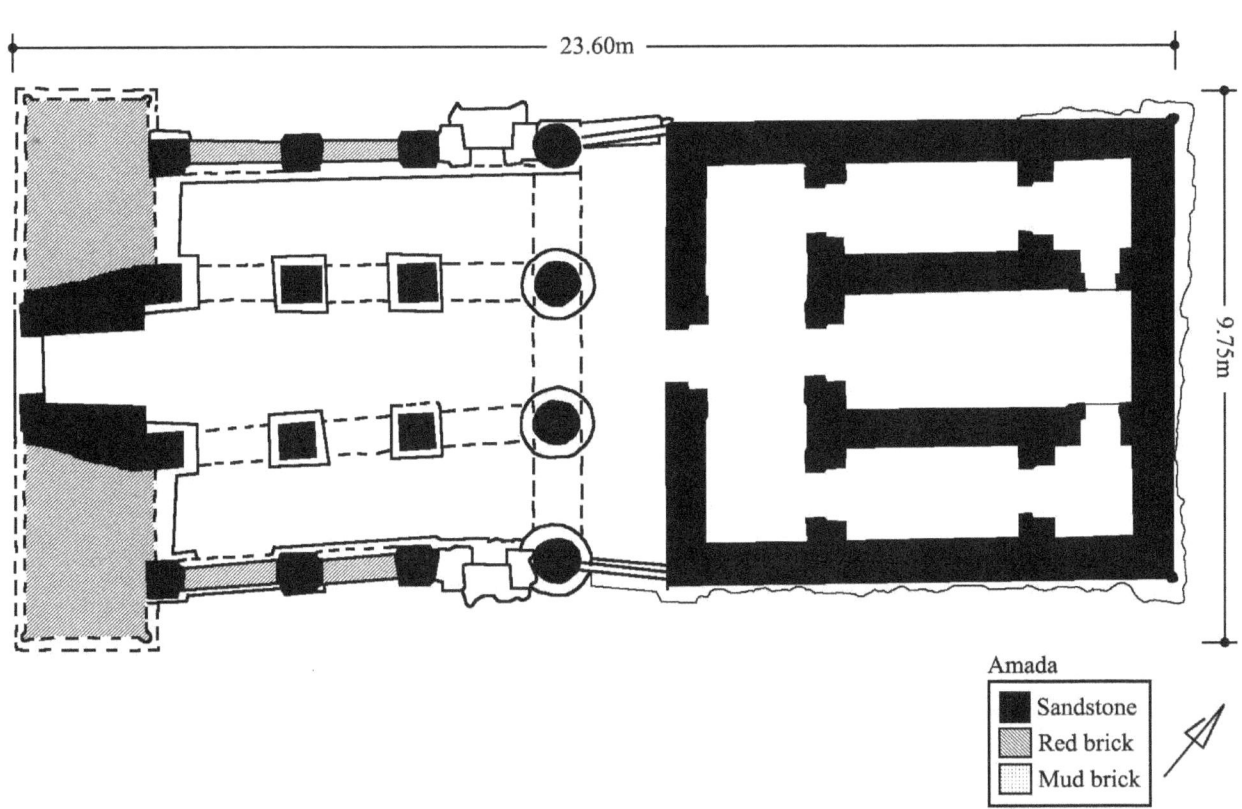

ANIBA, Lower Nubia (Egypt)
GPS (DMS): 22.40N 32.01E / Left bank
[Miam]

Postulated Temple of Amun

Period: New Kingdom

Brief Architectural Description:
N/A

Select Bibliographical References:
Barguet *et al.* 1967: 31; Guermeur 2005: 490-491.

QASR IBRIM, Lower Nubia (Egypt)
GPS (DMS): 22.39N 32.00E / Right bank
[Primis]

Postulated Temple

Period:	New Kingdom, Dyn. 20
Builder(s):	Ramses IV

Brief Architectural Description:
N/A

Select Bibliographical References:
Alexander 1999: 47-59; Plumley 1964: 3-5.

GEBEL ADDA, Lower Nubia (Egypt)
GPS (DMS): 22.18N 31.34E / Right bank

Meroitic Temple (dedicated to Amun?)

Period:	Meroitic
Builder(s):	Unknown
Orientation:	South-north
Measurements:	Not published [N/A]
Construction materials:	Sandstone
Preservation status:	About three courses of blocks, foundation levels.

Brief Architectural Description:
The temple plan shows an open area walled only on two sides (destroyed temenos?). The main doorway leads to a large outer court and then to a court with perambulatory shrine in the centre and three chambers on each side. An elongated court adjacent to the outer court is only accessible from one of the small chambers.

Select Bibliographical References:
LÄ II: 433; Millet 1964: 153-159; 1967: 53-64; 1981: 111-122; 1984: 111-121.

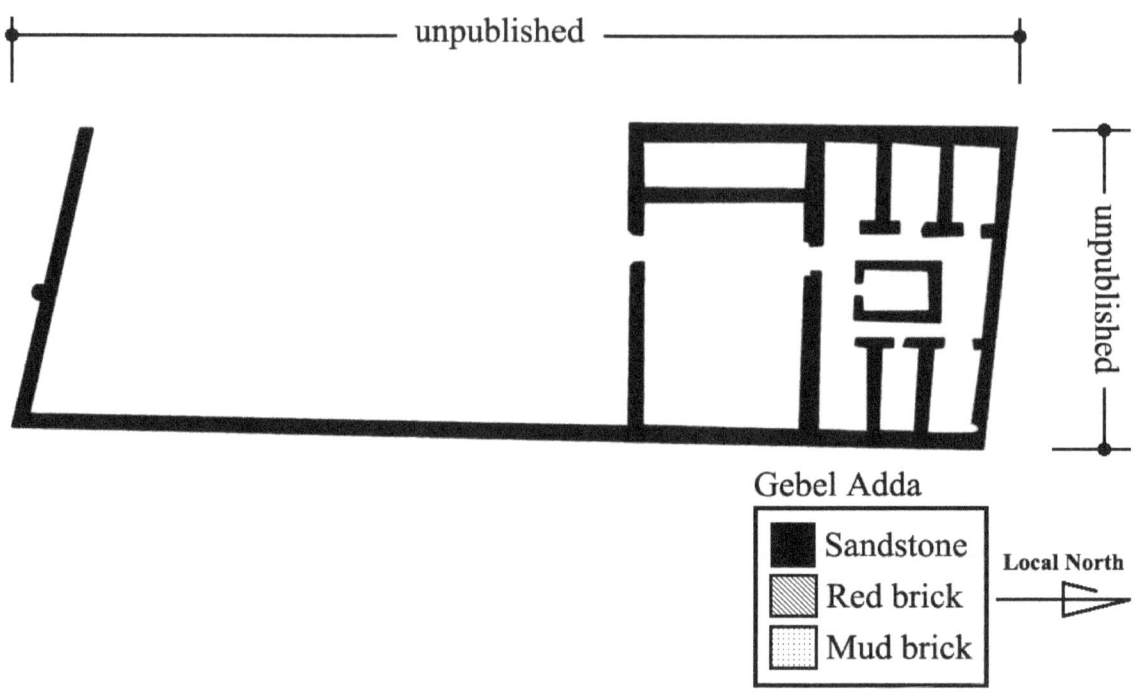

Figure 5: Gebel Adda, Meroitic Temple (Adapted from Millet 1968: 18.)

AKSHA, Lower Nubia (Sudan)
GPS (DMS): 22.10N 31.25E / Left bank (sections now in the National Museum, Khartoum)
[Serra West]

Temple of Amun, Rē, and the deified Ramses II

Period:	New Kingdom, Dyn. 19
Builder(s):	Ramses II
Orientation:	East-west
Measurements:	31* x 18.70 metres* [c]
Construction materials:	Sandstone, mud brick (temenos)
Preservation status:	Approximately 2 metres high.

Brief Architectural Description:
A pylon leads to a peristyle court (pillars on three sides only) with three gates opening towards the exterior of the temple. The next room is a vestibule that introduces three sanctuaries and two long and narrow chambers *en enfilade* on the south sanctuary area.

Select Bibliographical References:
Arnold 1992: 77; 2003: 7; Guermeur 2005: 494ff; Hein 1991: 38- 40; PM VII: 127-128; Rosenvasser 1964: 96-101; Vercoutter 1962a: 109-117; 1963: 131-140.

Figure 6: Aksha, Temple of Amun, Rē, and the deified Ramses II
(Adapted from Hein 1991: 194.)

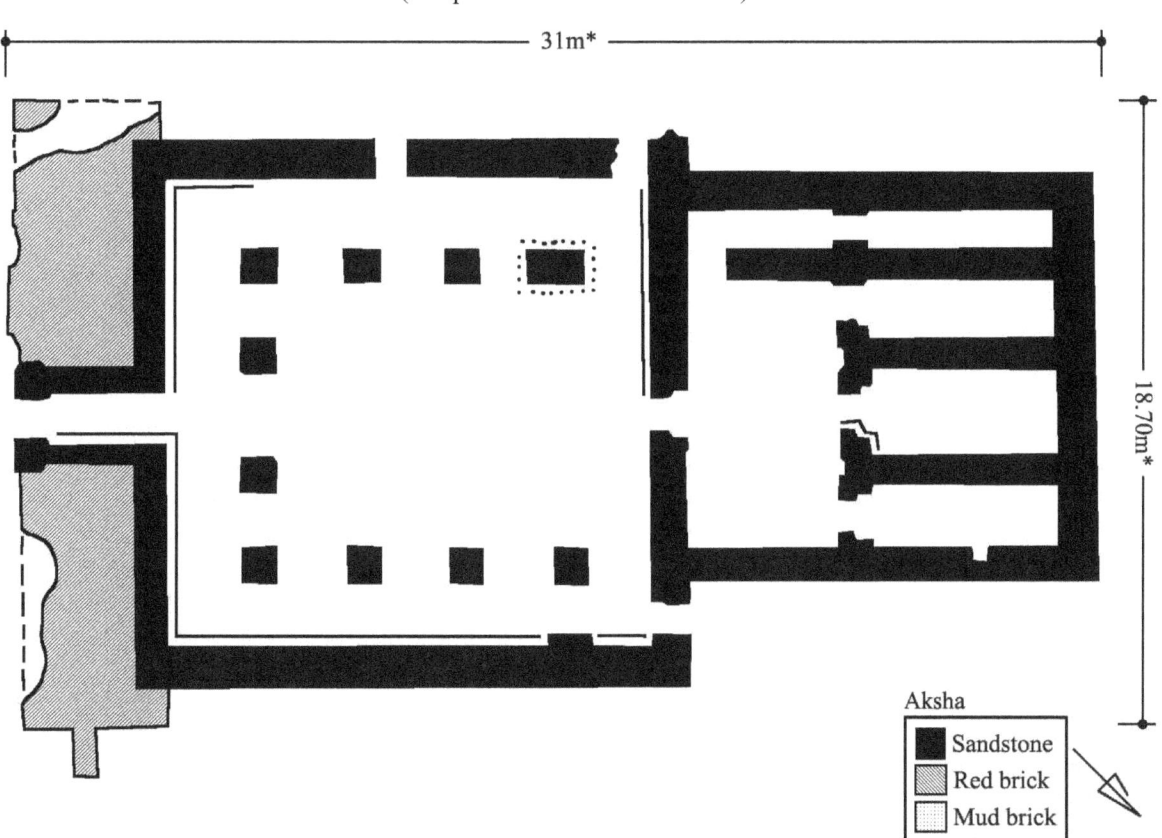

AMARA EAST, Abri-Delgo Reach (Sudan)
GPS (DMS): 20.48N 30.23E / Right bank

Temple of Amun

Period:	Meroitic
Builder(s):	Natakamani and Amanitore (with Prince Sherkarer)
Orientation:	North-south (?)
Measurements:	~14* x ~21 metres* (ruins of the remaining halls / incomplete) [c]
Construction materials:	Red brick, mud brick, sandstone, granite
Preservation status:	Destroyed between 1860 and 1905.

Brief Architectural Description:
Very little is left of this building. Lepsius noted a small hypostyle hall with doors at either end; one appears to lead into another similar hypostyle hall, while the other could lead into a larger hall or towards the sanctuary area.

Select Bibliographical References:
Hakem 1988: 333-336; Kirwan 1936: 101; LD I: 115; PM VII 1970: 157; REM: 0084 + 0144-0150; Wenig 1977.

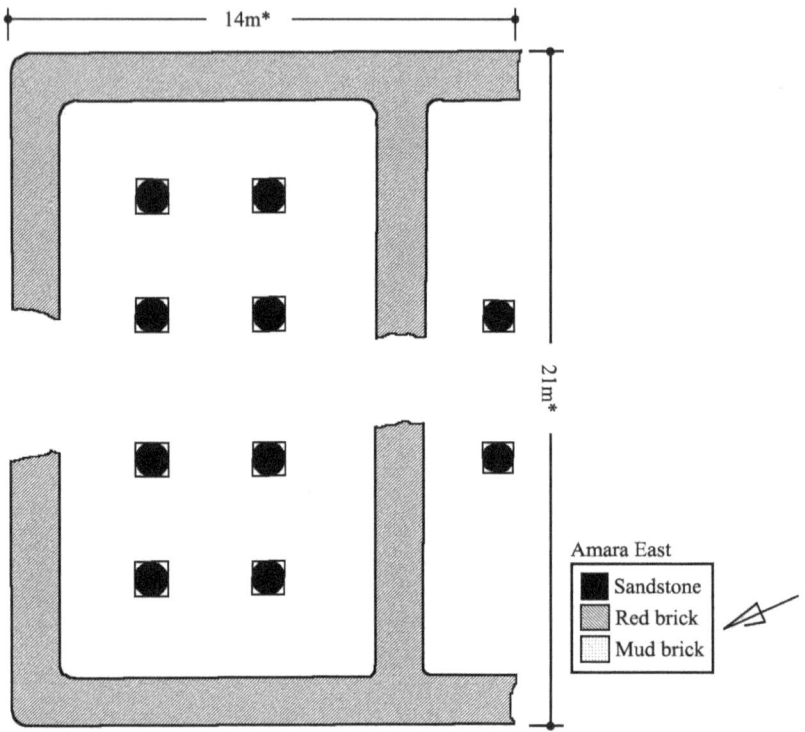

Figure 7: Amara East, Temple of Amun
(Adapted from Lepsius in Wenig 1977: 460.)

AMARA WEST, Abri-Delgo Reach (Sudan)
GPS (DMS): 20.45N 30.24E / Left bank

Temple of Amun-Rē

Period:	New Kingdom, Dyn. 19 and 20
Builder(s):	Seti I (temenos); Ramses II (temple); repairs and inscriptions by Merenptah, Amenmose, Ramses III, Ramses VI, and Ramses IX
Orientation:	North-south (final stage of the temple)
Measurements:	66.07 x 26.50 metres (from north wall of forecourt to back of the temple x maximum width of forecourt) [c]
Construction materials:	Sandstone, brick (temenos and forecourt)
Preservation status:	Approximately 2 metres high, full figures (minus headdress) are preserved in some locations.

Brief Architectural Description:
Without a pylon, the temple is entered from three gates leading to a large forecourt and the temple entrance is part of a thick temenos wall in front of which the forecourt was built. The first court behind the thick wall is a peristyle court with two exits, one of which leads to a small chapel. The next room is a small hypostyle hall of 12 columns that leads to a vestibule that gives access to three sanctuaries as well as a staircase on the west side.

Select Bibliographical References:
Arnold 1992: 74-75; 2003: 9; Fairman 1938: 151-156; 1939: 139-144; Guermeur 2005: 496ff; Hein 1991: 51-57; LÄ I 171-172; Spencer 1997.

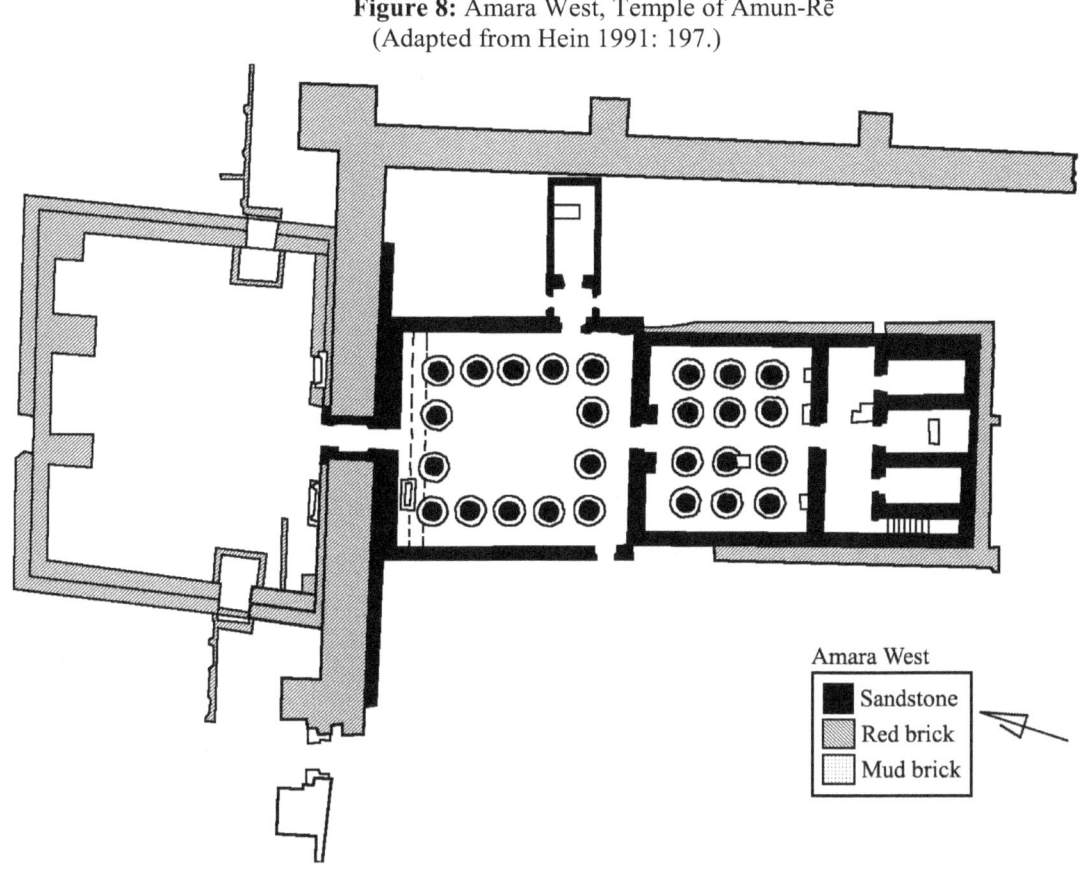

Figure 8: Amara West, Temple of Amun-Rē
(Adapted from Hein 1991: 197.)

SAI ISLAND, Abri-Delgo Reach (Sudan)
GPS (DMS): 20.42N 30.20E / Island

Temple A

Period:	New Kingdom, Dyn. 18
Builder(s):	Thutmosis III
Orientation:	East-west
Measurements:	13* x 10.5 metres* (incomplete) [c]
Construction materials:	Sandstone
Preservation status:	Foundation levels of sanctuary, front halls destroyed.

Brief Architectural Description:
The front of the temple is completely destroyed and all that remains is a triple sanctuary that was likely accessed from a vestibule.

Select Bibliographical References:
Arnold 2003: 9; Hein 1991: 58-60; LÄ V: 353-354; PM VII: 164-5; Vercoutter 1956: 66-82; 1958: 144-68; 1973: 9-38; 1974: 28-36.

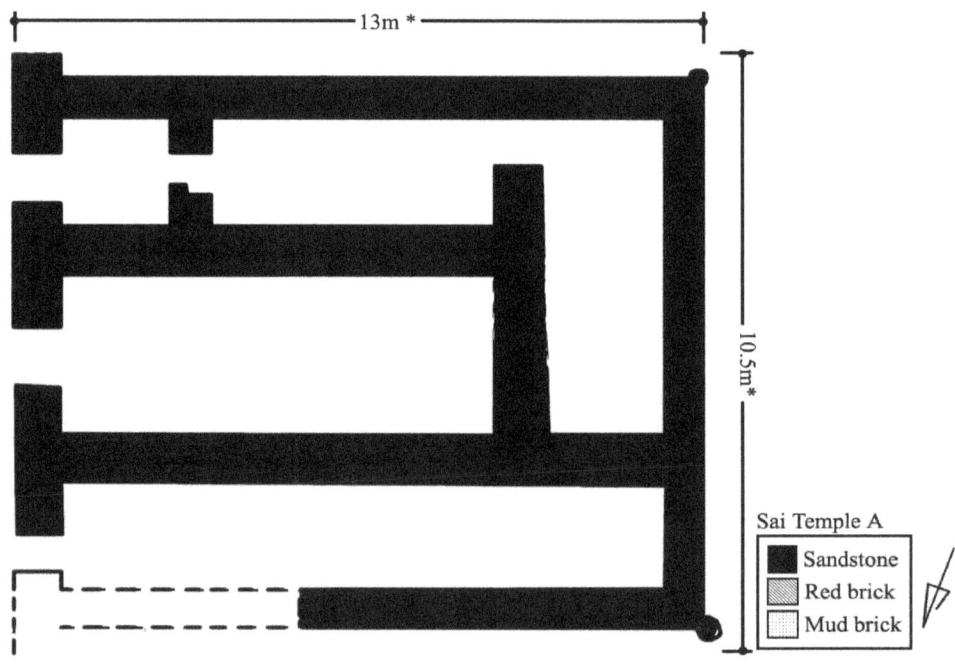

Figure 9: Sai Island, Temple A
(Adapted from Vercoutter 1973: 9-38.)

SOLEB, Abri-Delgo Reach (Sudan)
GPS (DMS): 20.27N 30.20E / Left bank

Temple of Amun and Nebmaatrē as his "living image"

Period:	New Kingdom, Dyn. 18
Builder(s):	Amenhotep III
Orientation:	East-west, facing the Nile River
Measurements:	130 x 51 metres [c]
Construction materials:	Sandstone, granite
Preservation status:	Some columns are 14 metres high, but the sanctuaries are destroyed.

Brief Architectural Description:
The temple complex at Soleb is quite elaborate. The features that interest us start past the larger temenos wall. An avenue of rams, lions, and obelisks leads to a portico and a previous temenos gate that acts as a pylon gate for the first peristyle court, the *heb-sed* hall. The next court, which would have been fronted by the pylon of a temenos of an earlier phase, is the sun court, a peristyle with two sets of columns on three of the sides. Next, a hypostyle hall leads to three columned sanctuaries, each with a small back room *en enfilade*. The central sanctuary is larger than the side ones and contains a shrine.

Select Bibliographical References:
Arnold 1992: 73-75; 2003: 224-225; Badawy 1968: 279-280; Baines and Málek 1980: 187; Guermeur 2005: 498ff; Hein 1991: 60-61; LÄ V: 1076-1080; PM VII: 169-172; Schiff-Giorgini 1958: 82-98; 1959: 154-170; 1961: 182-197; 1962: 152-169; Schiff-Giorgini *et al.* 1998; 2002; 2003.

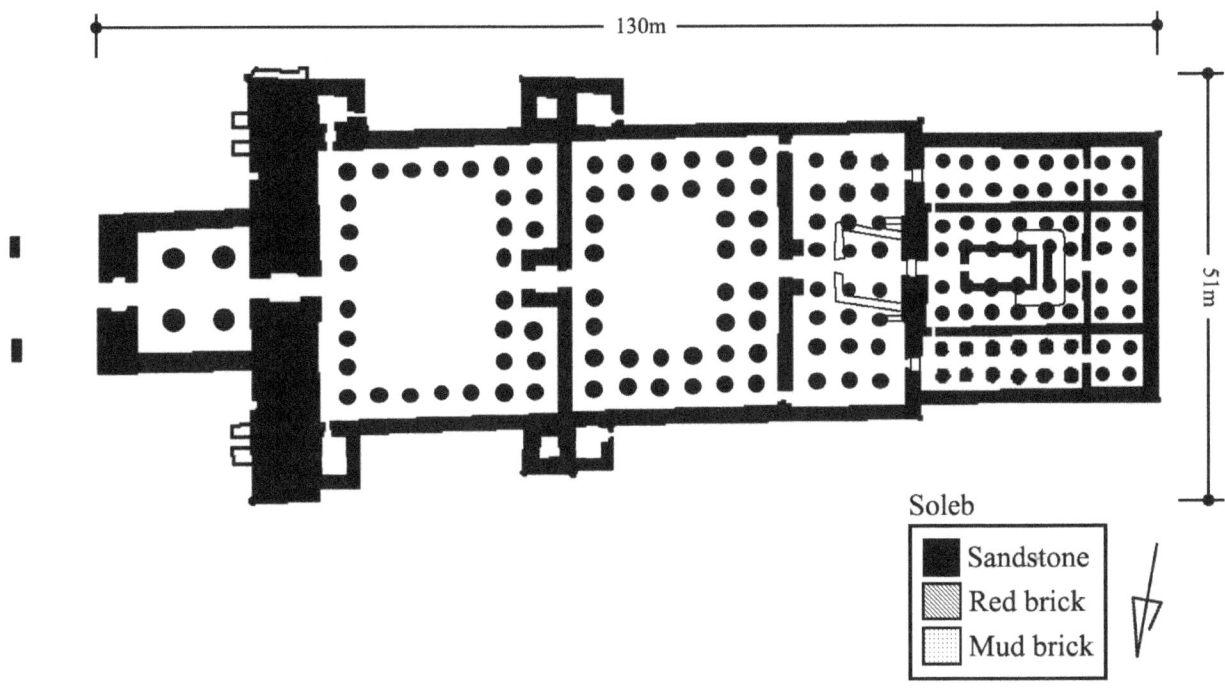

Figure 10: Soleb, Temple of Amun and Nebmaatrē
(Adapted from Schiff-Giorgini *et al.* 2003: 7, fig. 7.)

SESEBI, Abri-Delgo Reach (Sudan)
GPS (DMS): 20.08N 30.33E / Left bank
[Sudla]

Triple Temple of the Theban Triad (?)

Period:	New Kingdom, Dyn. 18 and 19
Builder(s):	Amenhotep IV, altered by Seti I
Orientation:	East-west
Measurements:	65* x 51 metres* [c]
Construction materials:	Sandstone
Preservation status:	Foundation levels, except for three full height columns.

Brief Architectural Description:
This temple has a unique plan, where a large open court leads to three small adjacent temples. The central temple has a wide hypostyle hall that leads into pronaos with columns on a podium. The sanctuary is a small room with access to the side temple sanctuaries. A niched sanctuary was later added behind this small sanctuary. The side temples follow the same pattern. The main court leads to a smaller open court that opens to a small columned pronaos and then a small sanctuary that connects with the main temple sanctuary from the side.

Select Bibliographical References:
Arnold 1992: 72; 2003: 219; Badawy 1968: 274; Blackman 1937: 145-151; Fairman 1938: 154; Hein 1991; 198; PM VII: 172-174.

Figure 11: Sesebi, Triple Temple of the Theban Triad (?)
(Adapted from Hein 1991: 198 and Arnold 2003: 219.)

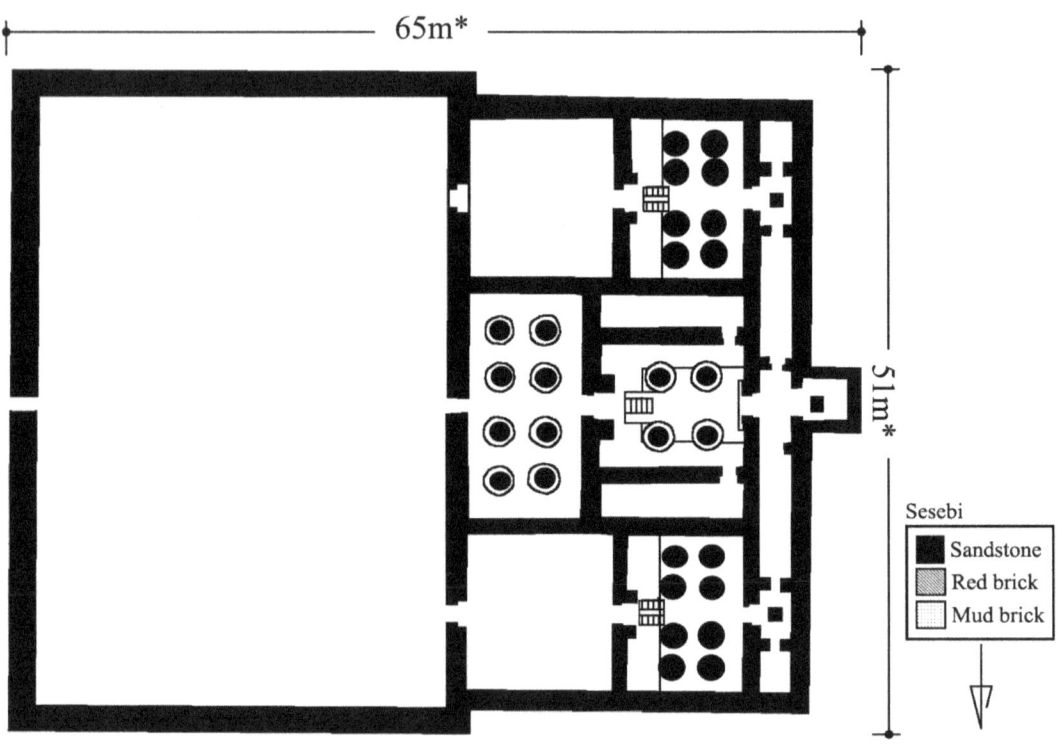

DOUKKI GEL, Dongola Reach (Sudan)
GPS (DMS): 19.26N 30.24E / Right bank
[*Kôm* des Bodegas]

Temple Complex of Amun of Pnubs: West Temple

Period:	New Kingdom, Dyn. 18
Builder(s):	Thutmosis IV (with the name of Thutmosis III in the south-west foundation deposit)
Orientation:	North-south
Measurements:	36 x 25 metres [c]
Construction materials:	Sandstone
Preservation status:	Foundation levels (a few centimetres only), flooring, negative impressions.

Brief Architectural Description:
The temple is accessed from a path coming from the ceremonial palace, right of the entrance. The facade was a wide pylon, which led into a small rectangular court with 4 columns, perhaps an open court. The following room is difficult to interpret; a central room flanked by two smaller lateral rooms on each side have been discovered below the foundations. These might be support structures to carry the weight of architraves. The next room is a wide pronaos that gives access to a small vestibule and tripartite sanctuary, each room identical in size. The base of a shrine was discovered in the sanctuary.

Select Bibliographical References:
Bonnet and Valbelle 2004: 109; 2005: 48-51.

Figure 12: Doukki Gel, Temple Complex of Amun of Pnubs, West Temple
(Adapted from Bonnet and Valbelle 2005: 48.)

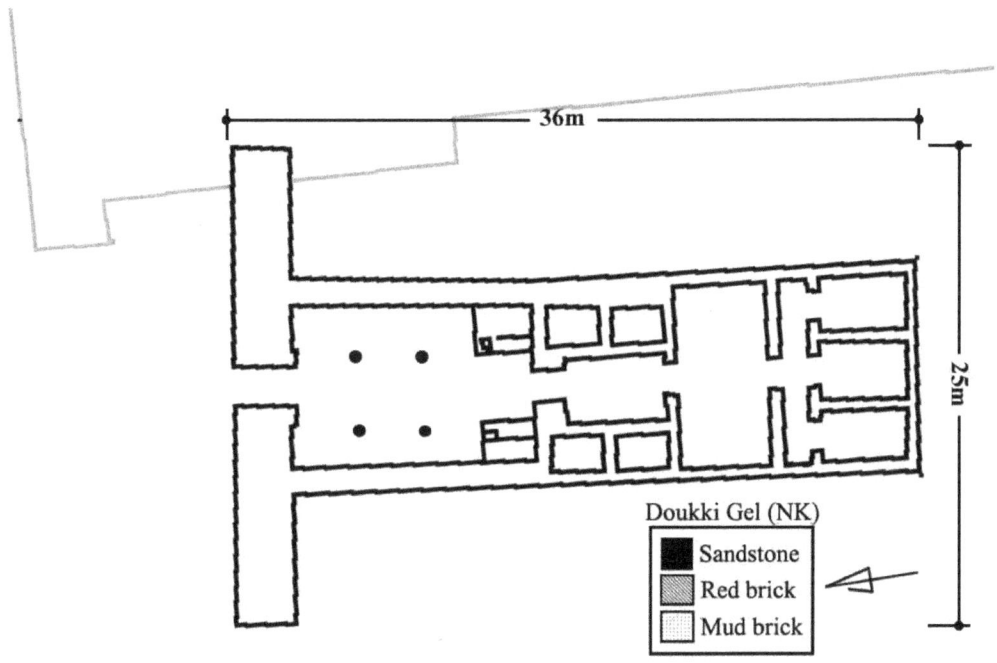

DOUKKI GEL, Dongola Reach (Sudan)
GPS (DMS): 19.26N 30.24E / Right bank
[Kôm des Bodegas]

Temple Complex of Amun of Pnubs: West Temple and Annexes

Period: Dyn. 25
Builder(s):   Unknown
Orientation: North-south
Measurements: 36 x ~ 45 metres [c]
Construction materials: Sandstone and mud brick
Preservation status: Foundations, negative impressions.

Brief Architectural Description:
Additions to the main building (above) are noted on both the east and west sides. A doorway, in the south-west corner, leads to a room off the main hall; another in the opposite corner leads to a columned hall and ultimately outside. These are *en enfilade* creating a second axis. From that east hall, a series of rooms can be accessed on both sides: two long and narrow rooms with perhaps a third very small one on the north, while south a north-south corridor leads to an L-shaped room. Another large room can be found on the east of the tripartite sanctuary; however, its access cannot be determined.

Select Bibliographical References:
Bonnet and Valbelle 2004: 110-111; 2005: 64-69.

Figure 13: Doukki Gel, Temple Complex of Amun of Pnubs, West Temple and Annexes (Adapted from Bonnet and Valbelle 2005: 65.)

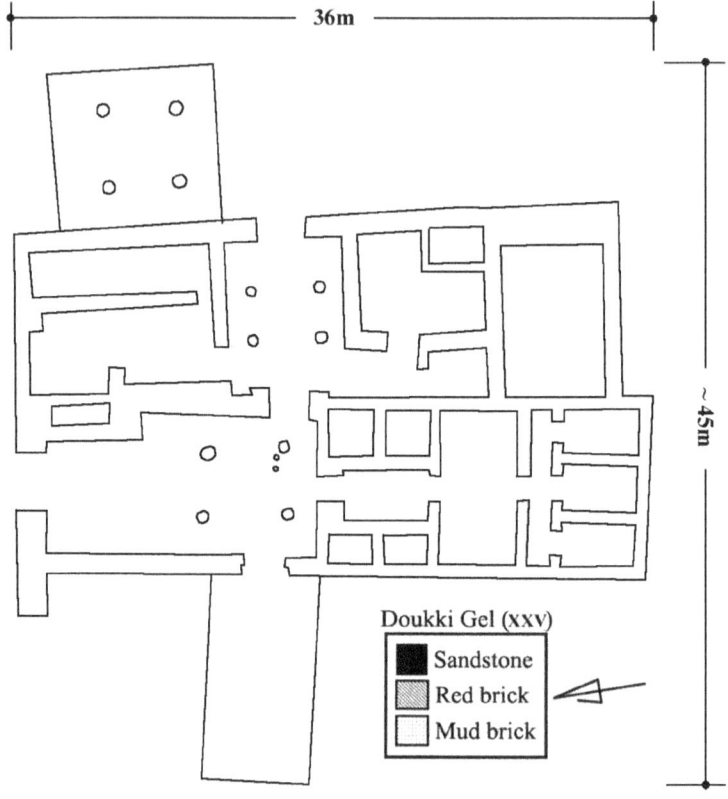

DOUKKI GEL, Dongola Reach (Sudan)
GPS (DMS): 19.26N 30.24E / Right bank
[*Kôm* des Bodegas]

Temple Complex of Amun of Pnubs: West and East Temples - Napatan phase

Period: Napatan
Builder(s):   Unknown
Orientation: North-south
Measurements: ~42 x ~52 metres [c]
Construction materials: Red bricks and mud bricks
Preservation status: Foundation levels, negative impression of first course, sanctuary destroyed.

Brief Architectural Description:
Two temples were built in the same location, east of the central annexes of the west temple. The first dates back to the Napatan period and is the smaller of the two. The pylon, which appears to be part of the temenos, leads to a small hypostyle hall with 4 columns. The next two rooms are of identical width and neither has columns. The first is aligned with rooms in the central annex and western temple in an east-west axis. Both earlier structures were incorporated into what might be called a temple multiplex. The sanctuary area is completely destroyed.

Select Bibliographical References:
Ahmed 1999: 39-46; Bonnet 1999: 57-76; 2001: 199-217; 2002: 35-44; Bonnet and Valbelle 2000: 1099-1120; 2005: 38-39; Valbelle and Bonnet 2003: 289-304.

Figure 14: Doukki Gel, Temple Complex of Amun of Pnubs, West and East Temples (Napatan) (Adapted from Bonnet and Valbelle 2005: 38.)

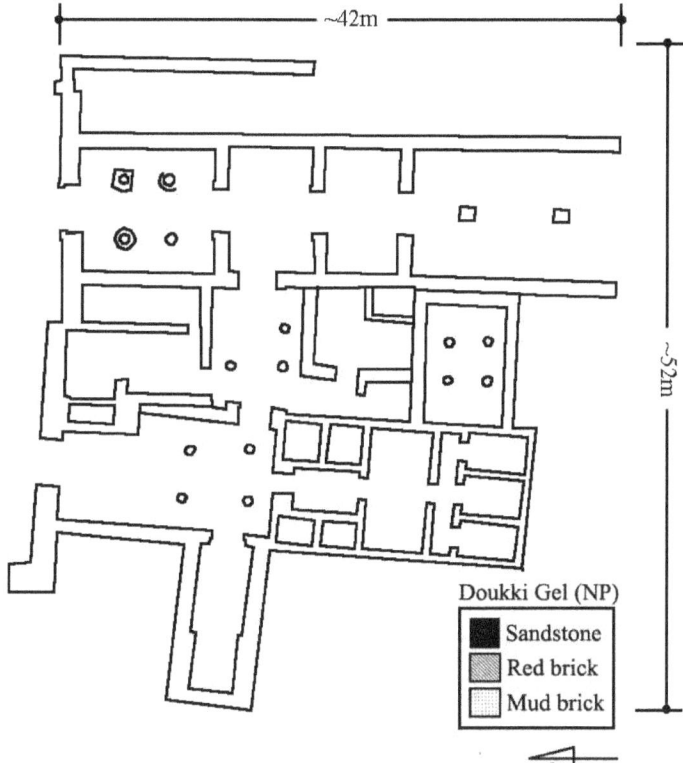

DOUKKI GEL, Dongola Reach (Sudan)
GPS (DMS): 19.26N 30.24E / Right bank
[*Kôm* des Bodegas]

Temple Complex of Amun of Pnubs: *West and East Temples - Meroitic Phase*

Period:	Meroitic
Builder(s):	Unknown
Orientation:	North-south
Measurements:	~45 x 52 metres [c]
Construction materials:	Red bricks and mud bricks
Preservation status:	Up to seven courses of bricks, sanctuary destroyed.

Brief Architectural Description:
A larger Meroitic temple was built over the Napatan East Temple. The pylon gives way to a 14-columned peristyle court with a water basin (?) in the south-west corner. The next room is a smaller hypostyle hall that is approximately the size of the two small rooms of the Napatan temple. The sanctuary area of the Meroitic temple is also destroyed. Two altars have been found in what is the supposed sanctuary area. The central annexes and the West Temple were maintained with only slight modifications to the earlier plan.

Select Bibliographical References:
Ahmed 1999: 39-46; 2004; Bonnet 1999: 57-76; 2001: 199-217; 2002: 35-44; Bonnet and Valbelle 2000: 1099-1120; 2004: 111-112, 2005: 40-41, Valbelle and Bonnet 2003: 289-304.

Figure 15: Doukki Gel, Temple Complex of Amun of Pnubs, West and East Temples (Meroitic)
(Adapted from Bonnet and Valbelle 2005: 40.)

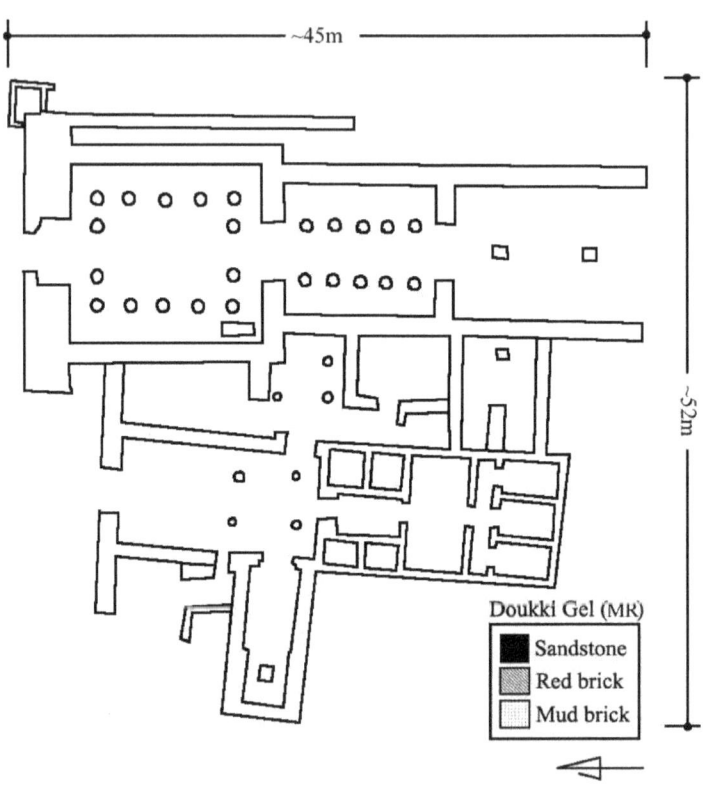

TABO (Argo Island), Dongola Reach (Sudan)
GPS (DMS): 19.33N 30.25E / Island

Postulated Temple of Amun of Pnubs (?)

Period: Dyn. 25
Builder(s): Taharqo
Orientation: East-west
Measurements: ~75.60 x 40 metres [c]
Construction materials: Sandstone
Preservation status: Foundation levels, completely destroyed past the hypostyle hall.

Brief Architectural Description:
Fronted by a pylon, the first room of this temple is a peristyle hall with two gates leading outside the temple proper. A kiosk is built in the centre of this room. The second pylon gives access to a hypostyle hall. The next rooms, the pronaos, sanctuary, and what might be interpreted as a dais room are completely destroyed and the architectural plan is only hypothetical.

Select Bibliographical References:
Arnold 2003: 237; Baines and Málek 1980: 187; Hein 1991: 63; Jacquet-Gordon *et al.* 1969: 103-111; Jacquet-Gordon 1999: 257-263; LÄ I: 434; Maystre 1968: 193-199; 1969: 5-12; 1986: 11-15; PM VII: 180.

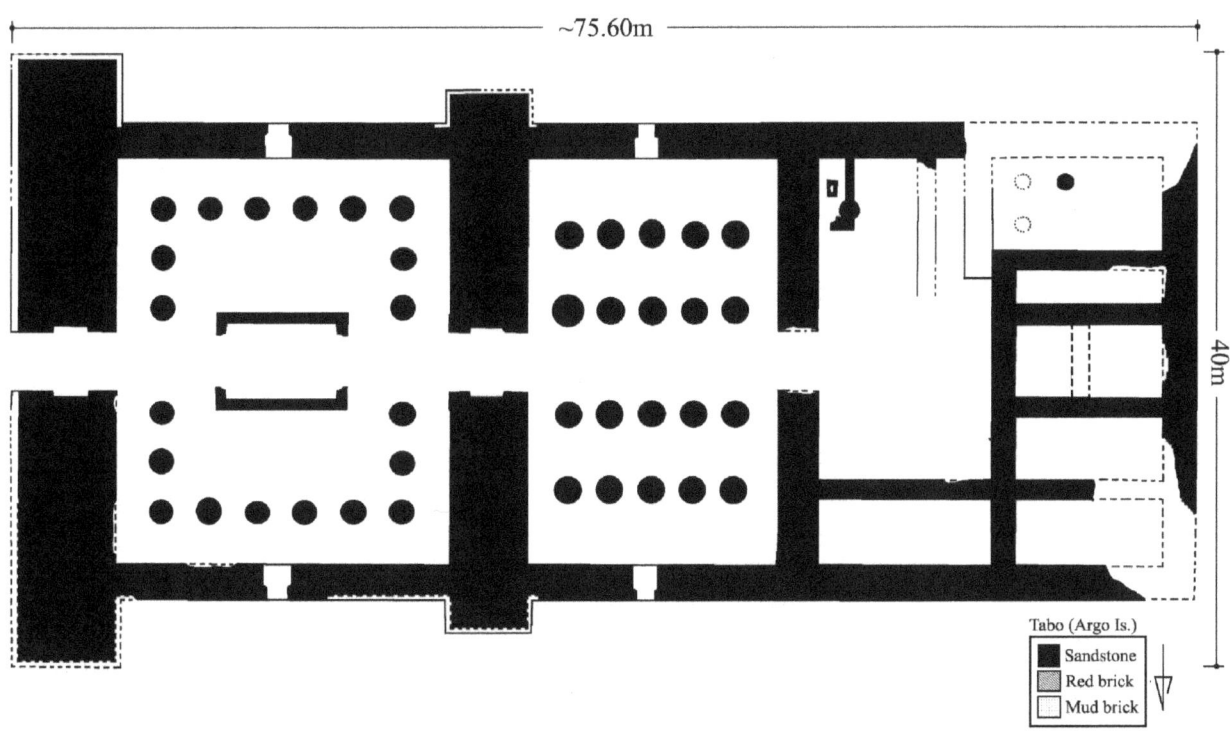

Figure 16: Tabo, Postulated Temple of Amun of Pnubs (?)
(Adapted from Maystre 1969: Pl. II and 1986: 14.)

KAWA, Dongola Reach (Sudan)
GPS (DMS): 19.07N 30.30E / Right bank
[Gematon, Gem-pa-Aten]

Temple A, Temple of Amun

Period:	New Kingdom, Dyn. 18
Builder(s):	Tutankhamun (perhaps on site of a temple by Amenhotep III), usurped by Ramses II, and enlarged by Taharqo
Orientation:	North-south, parallel to the river and perpendicular to the central axis of Temple T
Measurements:	38 x 17 metres [c]
Construction materials:	Mud brick and sandstone
Preservation status:	N/A

Brief Architectural Description:
Entrance to the temple is via a small portico and a portal, and into the first columned court. The second hypostyle hall, where altars are located, follows and leads into a very small pronaos built during an earlier period and integrated into the later building. This pronaos leads into small sanctuary as well as into side rooms, but the plan is not clear as to the exact configuration.

Select Bibliographical References:
Arnold 1992: 71; 2003: 102-121; Badawy 1968: 280-281; Guermeur 2005: 509ff; Griffith 1932: 87-89; LÄ III: 378; Macadam 1955; PM VII: 181-184.

Figure 17: Kawa, Temple A
(Adapted from Macadam 1955 [vol. II]: pl. 4.)

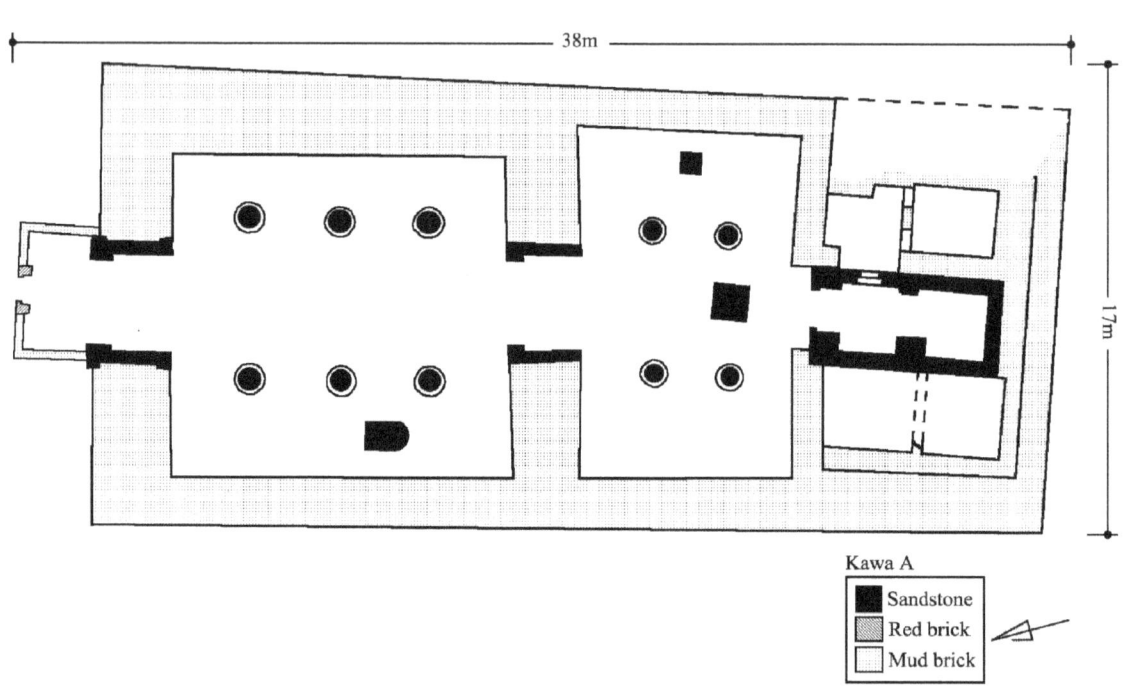

KAWA, Dongola Reach (Sudan)
GPS (DMS): 19.07N 30.30E / Right bank
[Gematon, Gem-pa-Aten]

Temple B, Temple of Amun

Period: Meroitic
Builder(s):   Unknown
Orientation: North-south, parallel to the river and at perpendicular to the central axis of Temple T
Measurements: 27 x 15 metres [?]
Construction materials: Sandstone
Preservation status: Columns are 2.64 m high.

Brief Architectural Description:
This small temple is built completely off-axis. The portal leads into the first court, which has only two columns. A second court with four columns follows. The second court leads into a large niched sanctuary as well as into a strangely shaped side room on the east side.

Select Bibliographical References:
Baines and Málek 1980: 187; Macadam 1955; PM VII: 184.

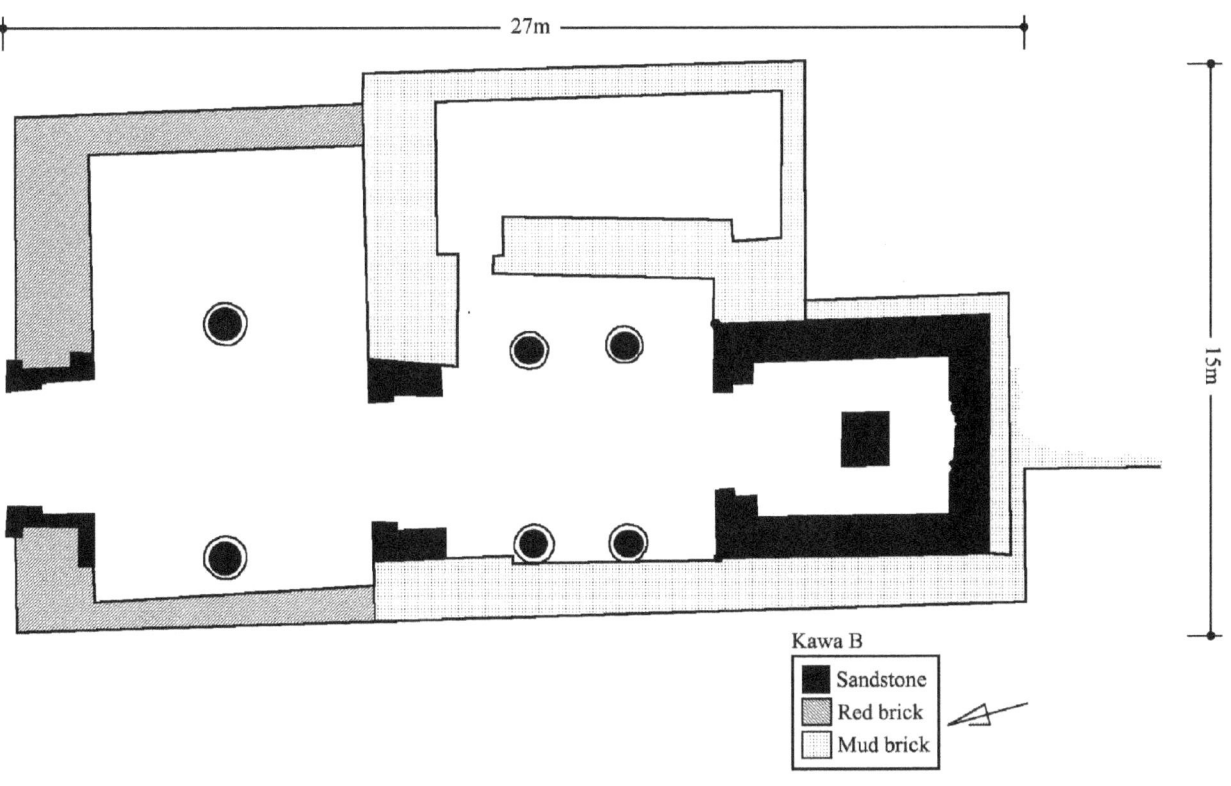

Figure 18: Kawa, Temple B
(Adapted from Macadam 1955 [vol. II]: pl. 4.)

KAWA, Dongola Reach (Sudan)
GPS (DMS): 19.07N 30.30E / Right bank
[Gematon, Gem-pa-Aten]

Temple T, Temple of Amun of Gematon

Period: Dyn. 25
Builder(s):   Taharqo
Orientation: West-east, facing the river
Measurements: 68.5 x 38.7 metres [c]
Construction materials: Sandstone and granite
Preservation status: Approximately 4 metres high.

Brief Architectural Description:
An avenue of rams leads to the first pylon, which reveals niches for flagstaffs. The first court is a peristyle with two side exits. A hypostyle hall, where two shrines are located, follows it. This hall leads to a pronaos with four columns, which then leads into the sanctuary as well as the dais room and columned hall on the south side, and a series of small chambers on the north side.

Select Bibliographical References:
Arnold 1992: 71; 2003: 120-121; Baines and Málek 1980: 187; Guermeur 2005: 511ff; Hakem 1988; Macadam 1955; PM VII: 184-191.

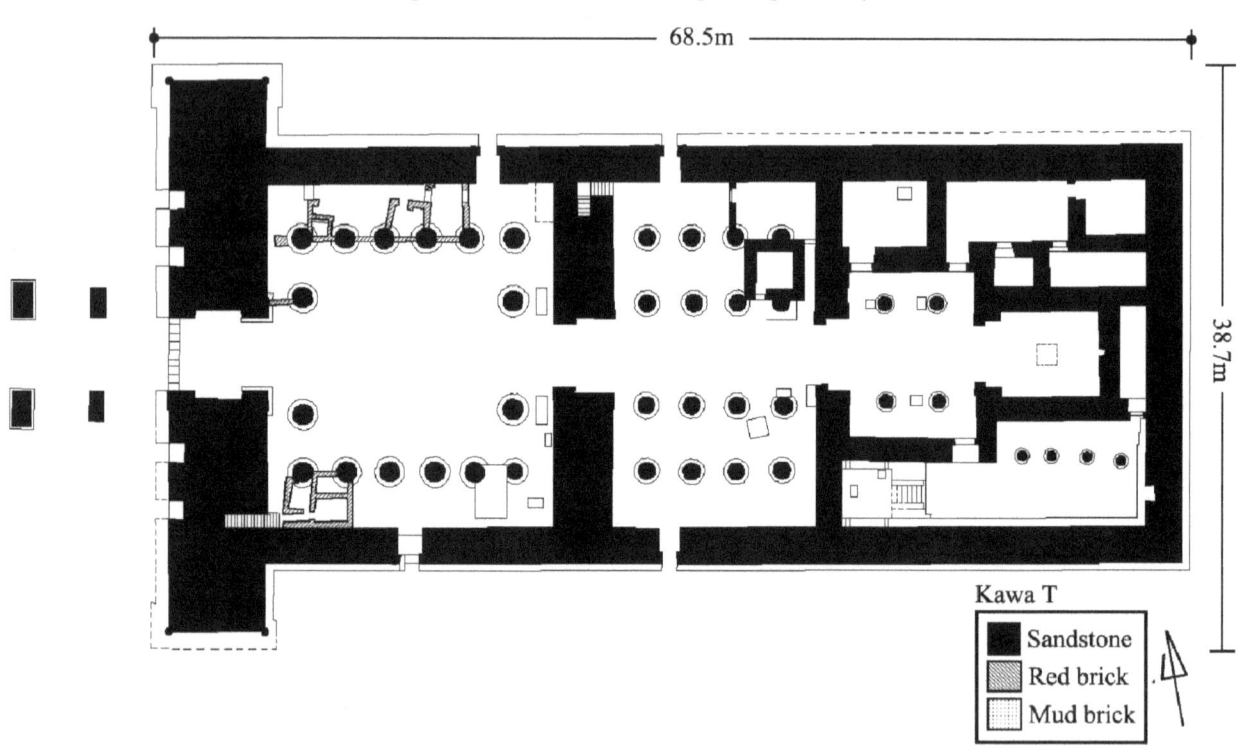

Figure 19: Kawa, Temple T
(Adapted from Macadam 1955 [vol. II]: 12-13.)

SONIYAT, Dongola Reach (Sudan)
GPS (DMS): 18.01.96N 31.05.99E / Right bank
[Tergis]

Temple TRG40, Napatan phase

Period: Napatan
Builder(s): Unknown
Orientation: South-north, facing the Nile River
Measurements: 30 x 19 metres [c]
Construction materials: Sandstone, lime mortar, and dovetail joints
Preservation status: Foundations, four to five courses of blocks.

Brief Architectural Description:
Two temples—Napatan and Meroitic—were built at the same emplacement. The Napatan temple is the larger of the two and consists of a main pylon that leads into a hypostyle hall with sixteen columns. This hall leads to two elongated side rooms as well as a small transverse vestibule, which in turn leads to the triple sanctuary. From the central sanctuary, a very small side room, which is located behind the east chamber, is accessible.

Select Bibliographical References:
Żurawski 1998: 149-160; 2001: 281-290; 2002: 217-226; 2003: 243-249.

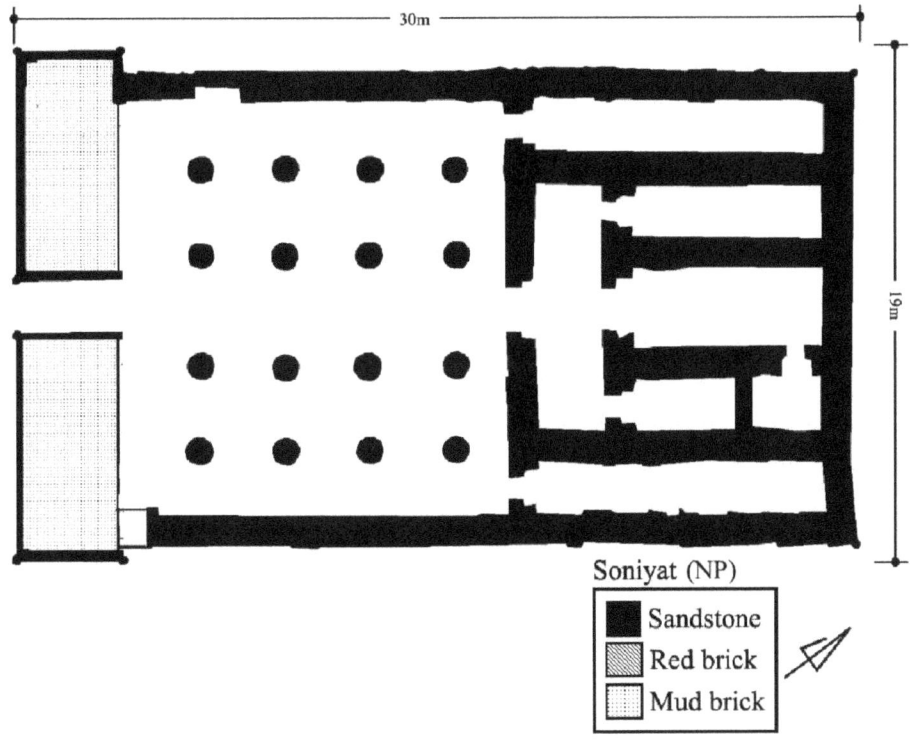

Figure 20: Soniyat, Temple TRG40, Napatan phase
(Adapted from Żurawski 2002: 218.)

SONIYAT, Dongola Reach (Sudan)
GPS (DMS): 18.01.96N 31.05.99E / Right bank
[Tergis]

Temple TRG40, Meroitic phase

Period: Meroitic
Builder(s): Unknown
Orientation: South-north, facing the Nile River
Measurements: 20.60 x 12 metres* [c]
Construction materials: Sandstone, lime mortar and dovetail joints
Preservation status: Foundations, four to five courses of blocks.

Brief Architectural Description:
A Meroitic temple was built at the same emplacement as the earlier Napatan structure. A pylon opens up to a small hall with four columns. The sanctuary configuration is the same as the Napatan temple: a vestibule and a triple sanctuary with a small side room, located behind the east chamber.

Select Bibliographical References:
Żurawski 1998: 149-160; 2001: 281-290; 2002: 217-226; 2003: 243-249.

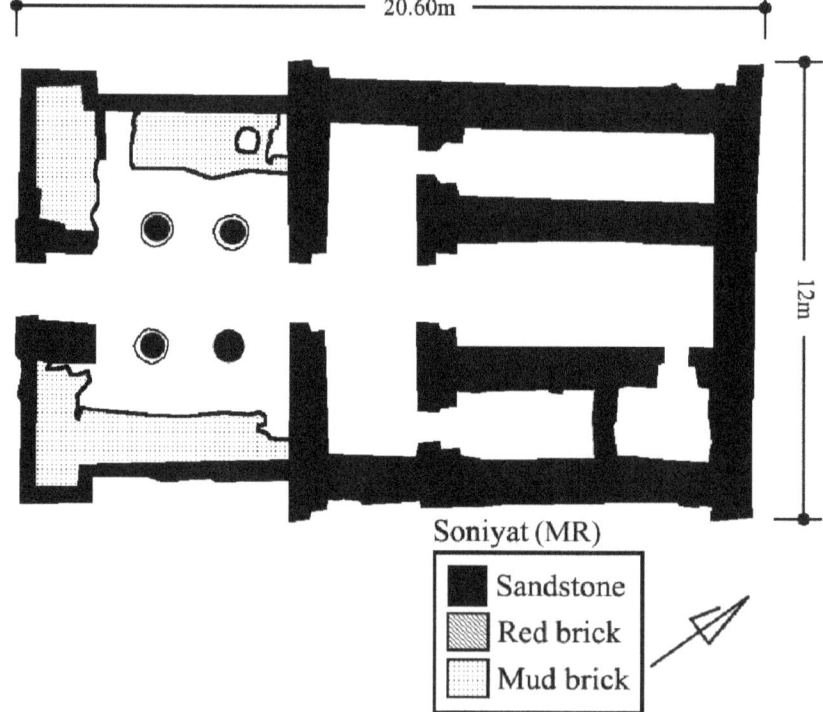

Figure 21: Soniyat, Temple TRG40, Meroitic phase
(Adapted from Żurawski 2002: 218.)

HUGEIR GUBLI, Dongola Reach (Sudan)
GPS (DMS): 18.14.40N 31.38.31E / Right bank
[Kerreri]

Postulated Temple of Amun of Tara-on-ensi

Period:	Napatan
Builders(s):	Harsiotef (?)
Orientation:	Facing the Nile River
Measurements:	~ 20 x 6.25 m [?]
Construction materials:	Sandstone
Preservation status:	Foundations of a destroyed sanctuary.

Brief Architectural Description:
Only a T-shaped block, most likely the entrance to the sanctuary, and a few other foundation blocks are visible. There is a column base *in situ*.

Select Bibliographical References:
Żurawski 2001: 281-290; 2003: 358-360; FHN II: 443.

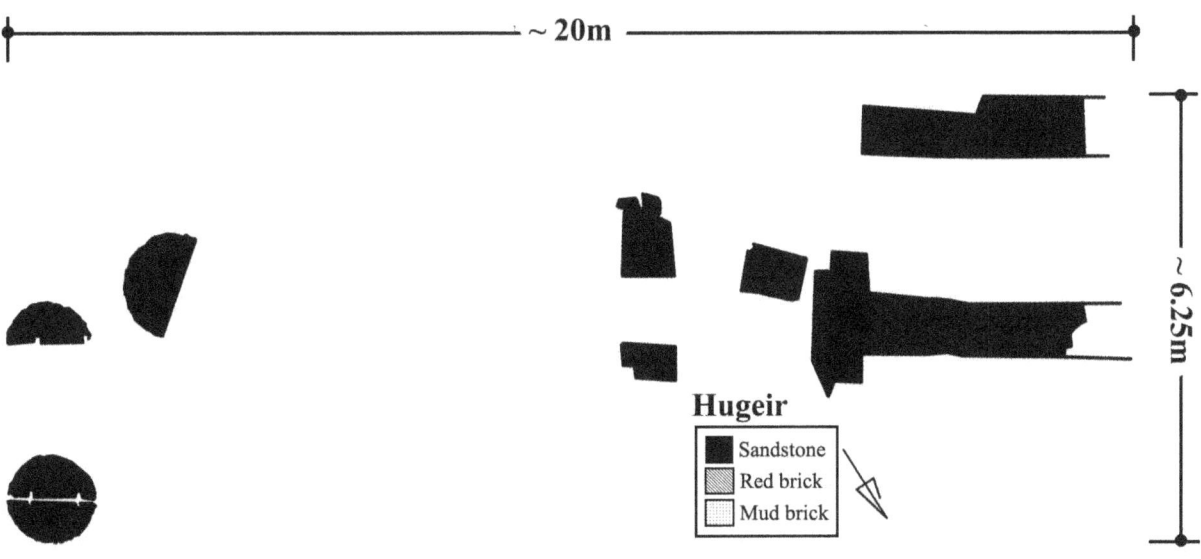

Figure 22: Hugeir Gubli, Postulated Temple of Amun of Tara-on-ensi
(Adapted from Żurawski 2003: 359, Fig. 3.)

SANAM ABU DOM, Dongola Reach (Sudan)
GPS (DMS): 18.27N 31.48E / Left bank
[Contra-Napata]

Temple of Amun, Bull of Nubia

Period:	Dyn. 25
Builder(s):	Taharqo
Orientation:	West-east, facing the Nile River
Measurements:	68.5 x 41.2 metres [c]
Construction materials:	Sandstone
Preservation status:	One or two stone courses above the floor.

Brief Architectural Description:
No sphinxes or rams have ever been found at Sanam. The entrance of this temple consists of a first pylon with flagstaff niches, which leads into a peristyle court with two side exits. The second pylon is slightly smaller and has no niches. It leads into a hypostyle hall with two side exits and two shrines. The next room is a pronaos with four columns that leads directly into the main sanctuary. From this pronaos, the dais room, a columned chamber, and a transverse room (behind the main sanctuary) can be accessed from the south. On the north, the pronaos gives access to five smaller chambers.

Select Bibliographical References:
Adams 1977: 174-175; Arnold 1992: 219; 2003: 208; Griffith 1922: 79-124; Guermeur 2005: 520ff; PM VII: 198-202.

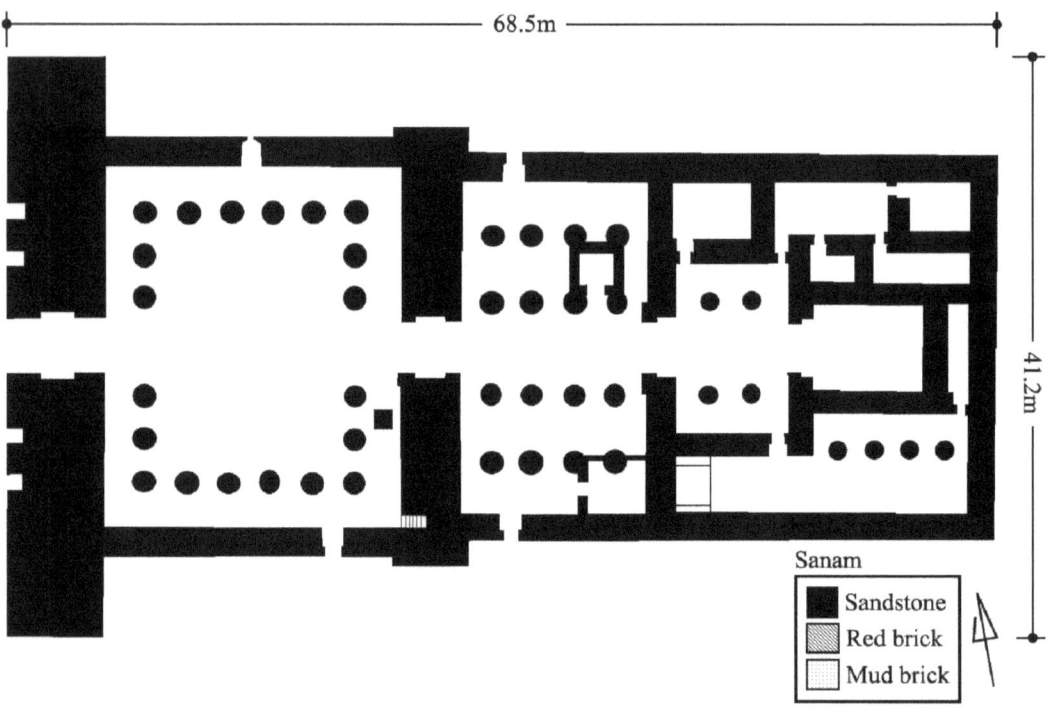

Figure 23: Sanam Abu Dom, Temple of Amun, Bull of Nubia
(Adapted from PM VII: 200.)

GEBEL BARKAL, Dongola Reach (Sudan)
GPS (DMS): 18.32N 31.49E / Right bank
[Napata]

Temple B500, Great Temple of Amun of Napata

Period:	New Kingdom, Dyn. 18 and 19, Dyn. 25/Napatan and Meroitic
Builder(s):	Tutankhamun/Horemheb, Ramses II, Piankhy, Taharqo, Tanwetamani, Amanishakheto, Amanitore and Natakamani.
Orientation:	East-west, facing the Nile River
Measurements:	150 x 46 metres [c]
Construction materials:	Sandstone, plaster, and granite
Preservation status:	Almost 2m, with reconstructed columns.

Brief Architectural Description:
An avenue of rams and a kiosk leads towards the first pylon. This pylon, with flagstaff niches and stairs, is the entrance to the peristyle hall, in which a second kiosk was erected. A second pylon with the same features follows, leading to a hypostyle hall that includes a third kiosk. The third pylon is smaller and leads into a columned hall that gives access to a small perpendicular room with an altar. A fourth pylon opens up to a columned court. In this court is located the entrance to the dais room, on the south side, and a small chapel on the north side. The next room is the vestibule that leads to the triple sanctuary.

Select Bibliographical References:
Arnold 1992: 89-90; 2003: 97-98; Dunham 1970; Guermeur 2005: 528ff; Hakem 1988: 107-130; Kendall: pre-print; 1992a; PM VII: 215-223; Reisner 1917.

Figure 24: Gebel Barkal, Temple B500
(Adapted from Hein 1991: 200.)

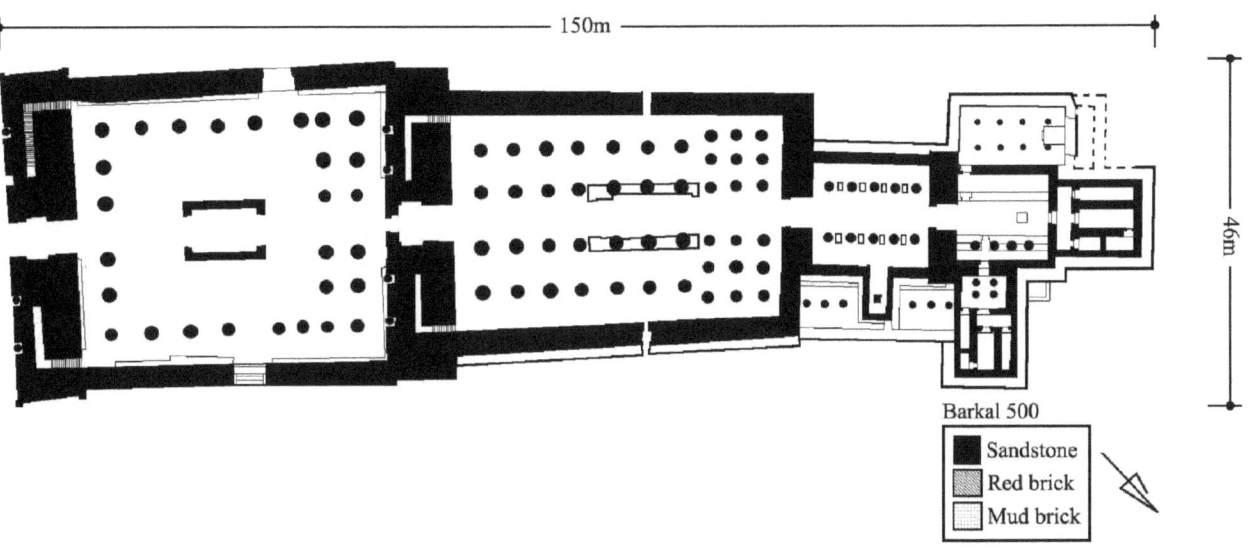

GEBEL BARKAL, Dongola Reach (Sudan)
GPS (DMS): 18.32N 31.49E / Right bank
[Napata]

Temple B700, Temple of Amun

Period: Napatan with Meroitic repairs and additions
Builder(s): Atlanersa, completed by Senkamanisken
Orientation: East-west, facing the Nile
Measurements: 32* x 20.5 metres* [c]
Construction materials: Sandstone, granite
Preservation status: Partially destroyed by a rock fall.

Brief Architectural Description:
The access to this small temple is via a portico with screens, inside which two columns are located. The main pylon that follows leads into a hypostyle hall with four columns. The next room also has four columns, and there is an altar in the temple axis. A small niched sanctuary with a small altar is located at the back of the temple.

Select Bibliographical References:
Arnold 1992: 90; 2003: 98; Dunham 1970; Kendall: pre-print; 1992a; PM VII: 213-215; Reisner 1918: 99-112.

Figure 25: Gebel Barkal, Temple B700
(Adapted from Dunham 1970, plan V.)

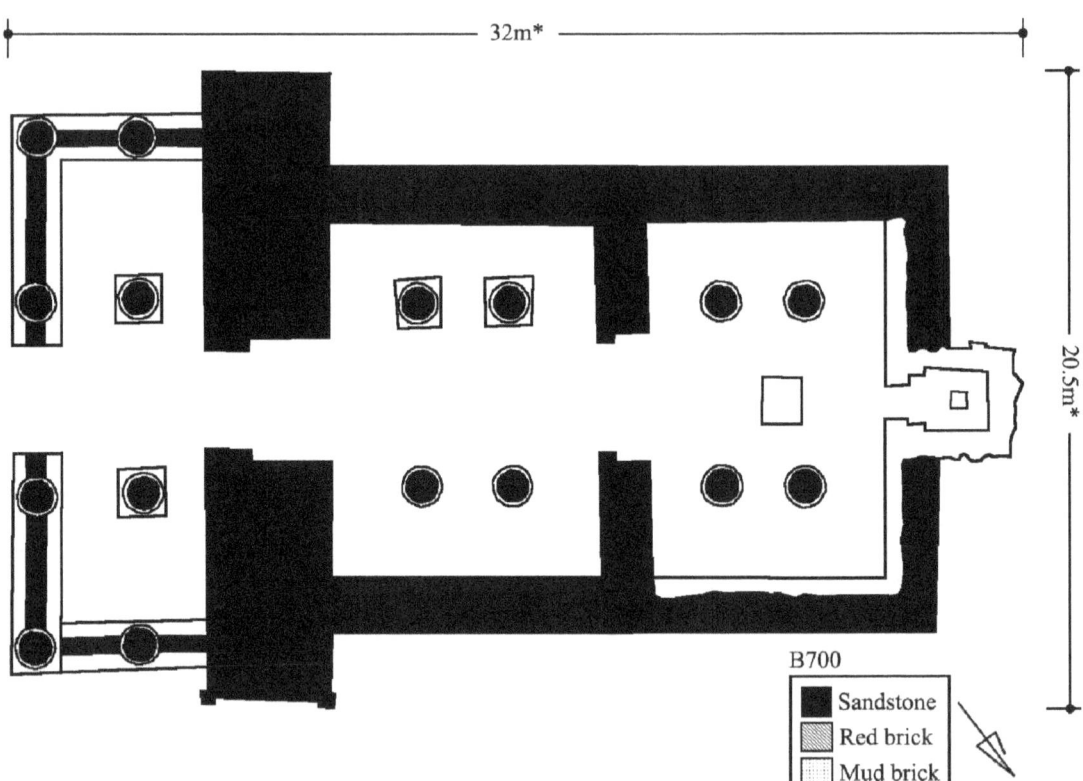

GEBEL BARKAL, Dongola Reach (Sudan)
GPS (DMS): 18.32N 31.49E / Right bank
[Napata]

Temple of Amun B800-First

Period:	Napatan and Meroitic
Builder(s):	Built by Kashta (or Piankhy), refurbished by Anlamani, destroyed during reign of Aspelta
Orientation:	East-west, facing the Nile River
Measurements:	55* x 31 metres* [c]
Construction materials:	Mud brick, sandstone, plaster
Preservation status:	Foundation levels.

Brief Architectural Description:
Two temples were built in the same location. The earlier building, called B800-First, has an entrance pylon followed by a hall with eight columns, leading into a court with six columns. From the north side of this court, a series of small rooms are accessible. The small hall that follows is completely off-axis. There are four columns and an altar within this room. The next room is a very small vestibule that leads to three sanctuaries.

Select Bibliographical References:
Dunham 1970; Hakem 1988: 144-149; Hofmann and Tomandl 1986: 25; Kendall 1992a: 141; PM VII: 212-213; Reisner 1920: 247-264.

Figure 26: Gebel Barkal, Temple B800-First
(Adapted from Dunham 1970, plan V.)

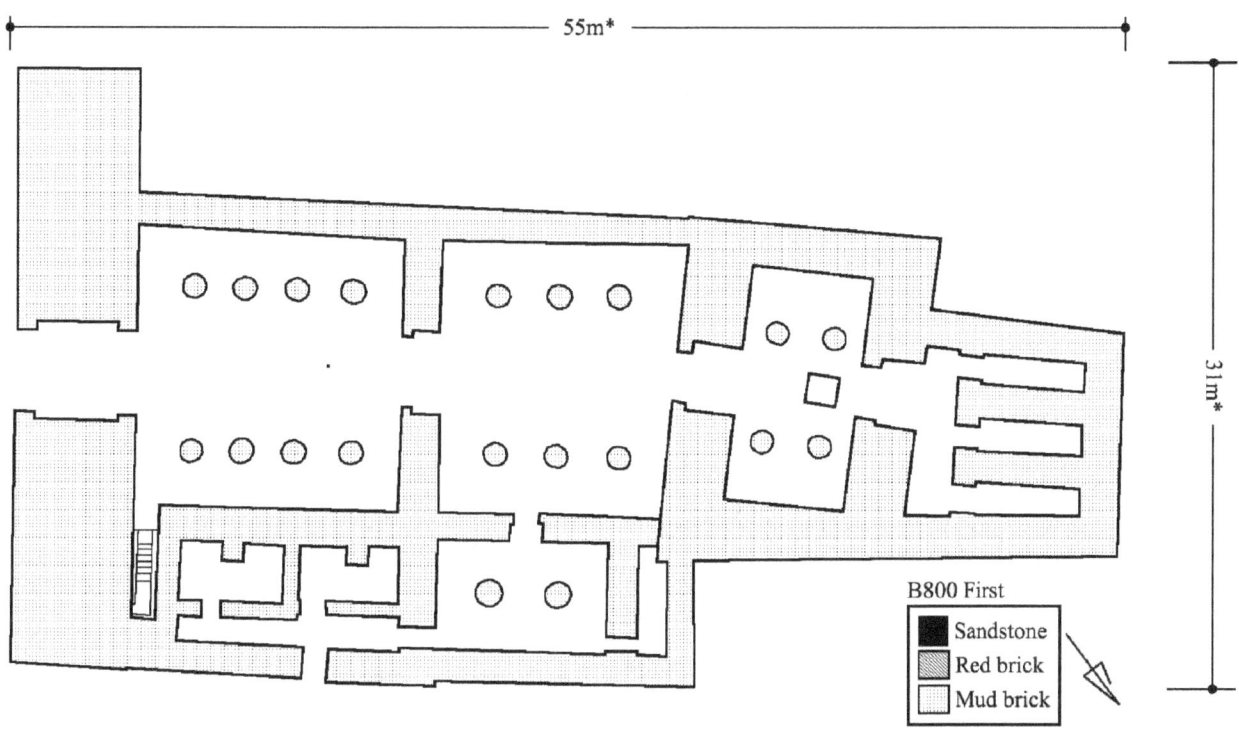

GEBEL BARKAL, Dongola Reach (Sudan)
GPS (DMS): 18.32N 31.49E / Right bank
[Napata]

Temple of Amun B800-Second

Period:	Napatan and Meroitic
Builder(s):	Built by Kashta (or Piankhy), refurbished by Anlamani, destroyed during reign of Aspelta
Orientation:	East-west, facing the Nile River
Measurements:	5* x 31 metres* [c]
Construction materials:	Mud brick, sandstone, plaster
Preservation status:	Foundation levels.

Brief Architectural Description:
Two temples were built in the same location. The later phase—B800-Second—also starts with a main pylon that leads into a court with six columns. The following hall is smaller, with only four columns. The pronaos, which is located where the third columned court appeared in B800-First, has four columns but no altar. It leads to a niched sanctuary with an altar. The temple is fronted by at least one pair of weather-worn ram statues.

Select Bibliographical References:
Dunham 1970; Hakem 1988: 144-149; Hofmann and Tomandl 1986: 25; Kendall 1992a: 141; PM VII: 212-213; Reisner 1920: 247-264.

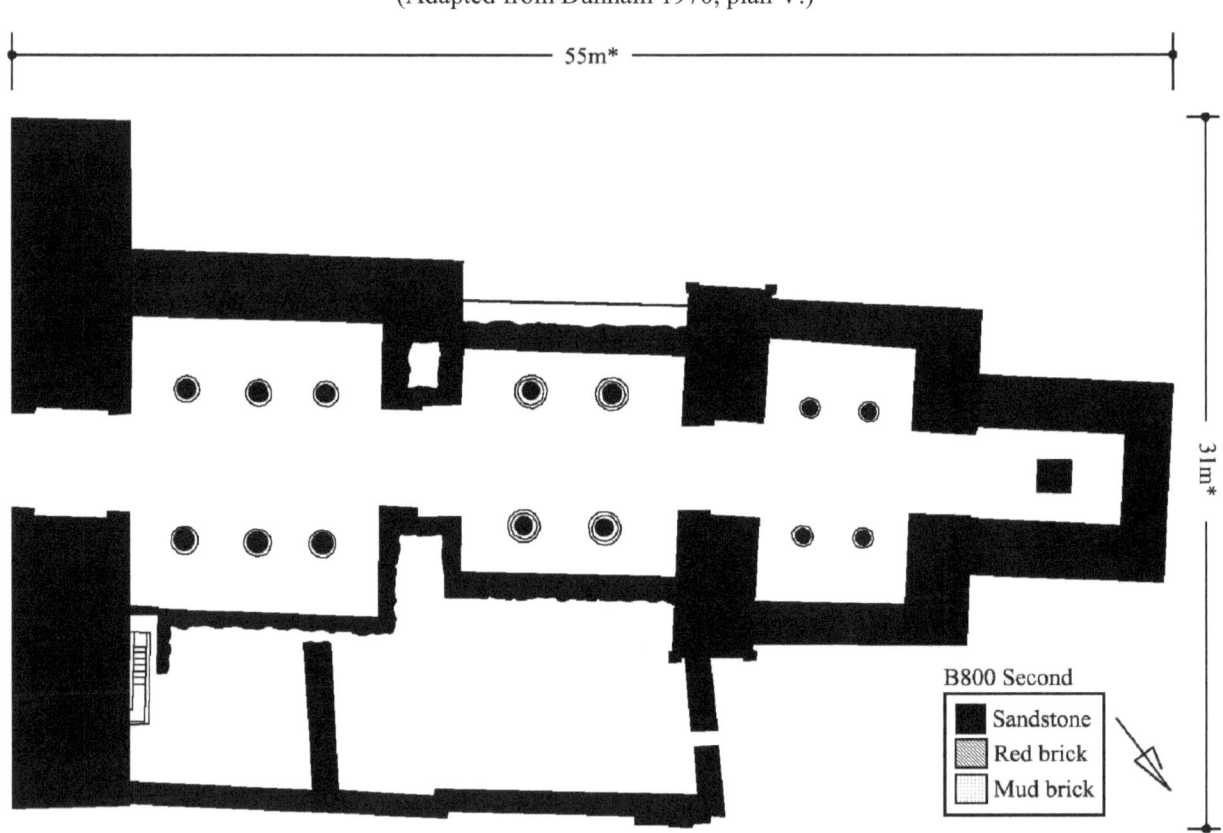

Figure 27: Gebel Barkal, Temple B800-Second
(Adapted from Dunham 1970, plan V.)

DANGEIL, Atbara-Khartoum Reach (Sudan)
GPS (DMS): 18.08N 33.58E / Right bank

Temple of Amun (Kôm H)

Period: Meroitic
Builder(s): Amanitore and Natakamani
Orientation: West-east, facing the Nile River
Measurements: 48.5 x est. 33.5 metres (not fully excavated) [c]
Construction materials: Red brick, mud brick, sandstone, and ferricrete
Preservation status: Walls are 1 to 3.5 m high.

Brief Architectural Description:
From a massive temenos gate, the temple is accessed via an avenue of ram statues and a kiosk. A portico stands in front of the main pylon. The first court is a transverse hypostyle hall with one exit on the north side. The next room is a smaller columned hall with six columns that leads to the pronaos, which has the same width, but only four columns. Two altars are found in this room. This pronaos gives access to a triple sanctuary. An altar, now destroyed was located in the central sanctuary. A door in the northern sanctuary leads to a long lateral room, the so-called dais room. The temple is only partially excavated.

Select Bibliographical References:
Ahmed and Anderson 2005; Anderson and Ahmed 2006a, 2006b, 2006-2007; Crowfoot 1911; Griffith 1911; PM VII: 233.

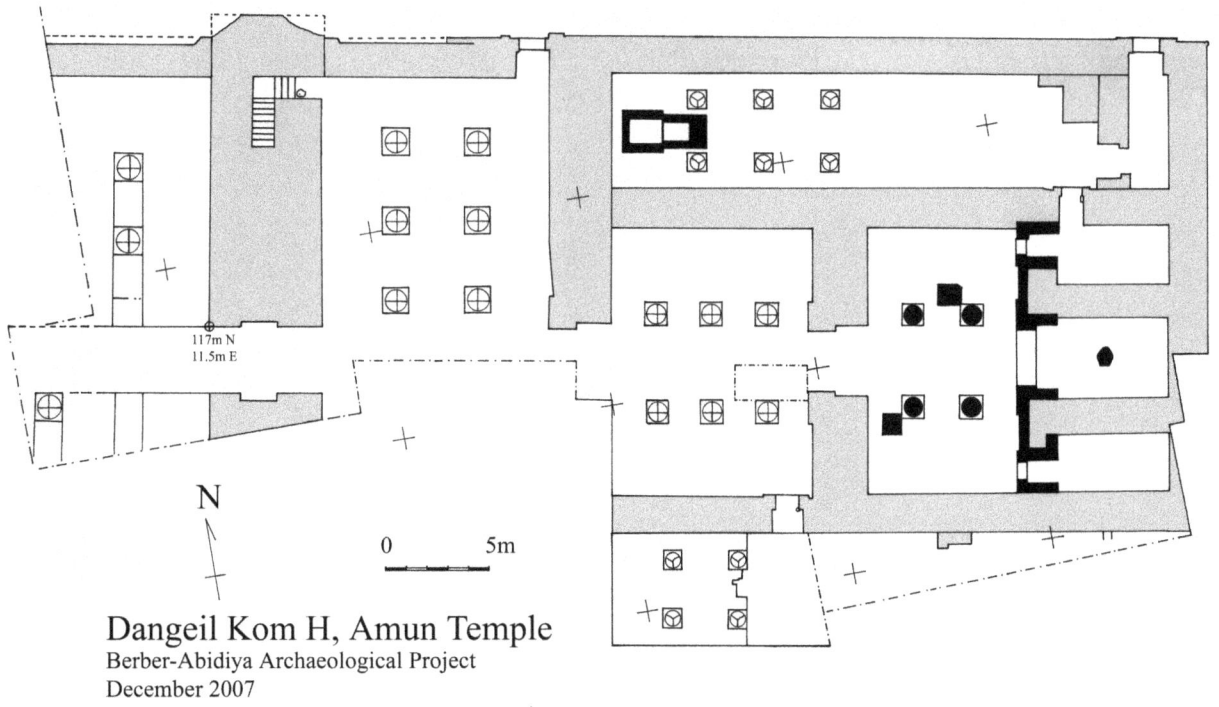

Figure 28: Dangeil, Temple of Amun
(Courtesy of the Berber-Abidiya Archaeological Project.)

MUTMIR, Atbara-Khartoum Reach (Sudan)
GPS (DMS): 17.06N 33.43E / Right bank
[Sakarage]

Postulated Temple

Period: Meroitic

Brief Architectural Description:
N/A

Select Bibliographical References:
Hinkel 2001; Hintze 1959: 174; Priese 1984c: 496; Zach and Tomandl 2000: 136.

MEROE, Atbara-Khartoum Reach (Sudan)
GPS (DMS): 16.54N 33.44E / Right bank

Temple KC104

Period: Meroitic
Builder(s): Cartouches of Amanitore and Arikankharor found painted on plaster
Orientation: North-south, perpendicular to M260's processional avenue
Measurements: 19.5 x 28 metres [N/A]
Construction materials: Sandstone, red brick, mud brick, and plaster.
Preservation status: Foundation levels.

Brief Architectural Description:
Two main entrances, both off the processional avenue of Temple M260, lead into the temple. Each doorway leads to a small hall of four columns and into a sanctuary with an altar. A series of rooms are located in the central portion of this double temple; however their access could not be determined due to the poor state of preservation. These consist of a long and narrow room and two transverse rear rooms, the southern most being divided into smaller rooms.

Select Bibliographical References:
Hofman and Tomandl 1986: 35; Shinnie 1984: 498ff; Shinnie and Anderson 2004: 56-62; Török 1997b: 518ff; Wenig 1984: 394; Zach and Tomandl 2000: 135-136.

Figure 29: Meroe, Temple KC104
(Adapted from Shinnie and Anderson 2004: pl. XIII.)

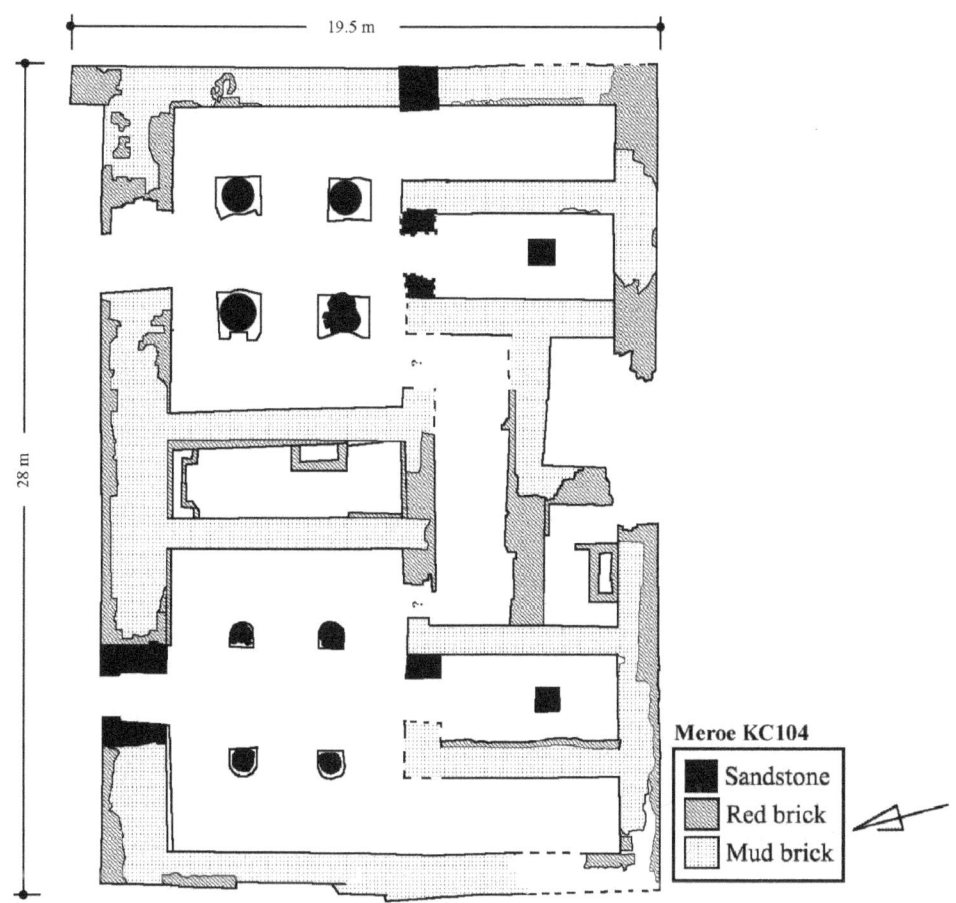

MEROE, Atbara-Khartoum Reach (Sudan)
GPS (DMS): 16.54N 33.44E / Right bank

Sun Temple M250

Period: Meroitic
Builder(s):   Aspelta, with repairs by Akinidad
Orientation: East-west
Measurements: 12 x 6.2 metres (internal) / 45 x 30 metres ("cloister") [c]
Construction materials: Sandstone, ferricrete
Preservation status: Approx. 1m high.

Brief Architectural Description:
Situated inside a temenos wall and surrounded by a peristyle colonnade with screens, the small temple is accessed via a ramp on its east side. A massive pylon is the entrance to the cloister, in which the small temple is located. Along the inner perimeter of the cloister is another colonnade. The small temple, located on another terrace, is accessed by a second ramp and a pylon. A small perambulatory shrine is located inside.

Select Bibliographical References:
Garstang 1910: 64-67; Hakem 1988: 191-213; Hinkel 2001; PM VII: 239; Shinnie 1967: 81-84; Török 1997a: 102-114; Welsby 1996: 120-122; Wolf 2006: 251-52; Zach 1999: 690-693.

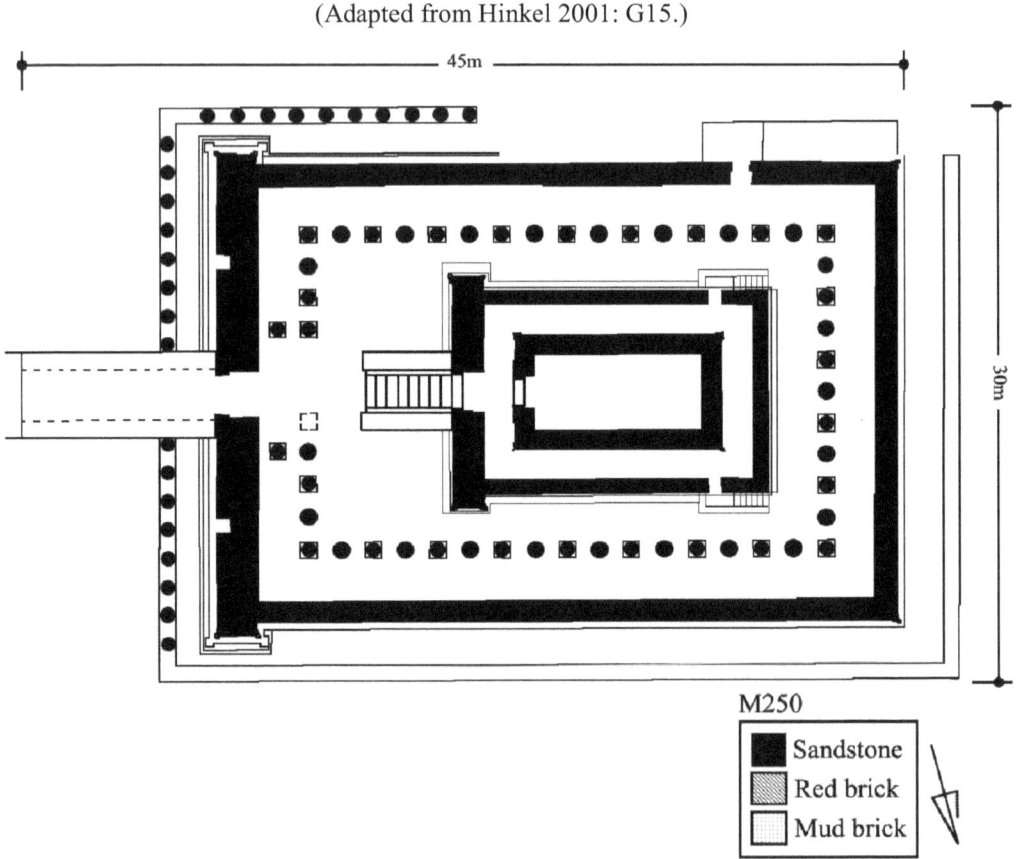

Figure 30: Meroe, Sun Temple M250
(Adapted from Hinkel 2001: G15.)

MEROE, Atbara-Khartoum Reach (Sudan)
GPS (DMS): 16.54N 33.44E / Right bank

Temple M260, Great Temple of Amun-Nete

Period:	Meroitic (with Napatan influences)
Builder(s):	Amanishakheto, Amanikhabale, Amanitore, and Natakamani
Orientation:	East-west, now facing the desert
Measurements:	114.76 x ~72 metres [c]
Construction materials:	Sandstone, red brick, mud brick, ferricrete
Preservation status:	Over 1m high.

Brief Architectural Description:
The approach to the temple is via a processional avenue of smaller temples, a kiosk, and ram statues. The first pylon leads to a long peristyle court with two exits and a second kiosk. A second pylon leads to a small hypostyle hall of eight columns with a ferricrete water basin along the axis and access to side rooms (?). A third pylon follows, leading into another small hypostyle hall that gives access to side chambers. The next room is the pronaos, where four columns and an altar are found. It gives direct access to the main sanctuary as well as numerous smaller rooms, including a dais room and a transverse room located behind the main sanctuary.

Select Bibliographical References:
Bradley 1984b; Garstang 1910: 57-70; 1911; 1912: 45-65; Grzymski, in preparation; 2003; Hakem 1988: 150-178; Hinkel 1997: 397-398, 399; Shinnie 1967: 77-78; Shinnie and Bradley 1980; Török 1997a: 116-128.

Figure 31: Meroe, Temple M260
(Courtesy of the Canadian-Sudanese Meroe Expedition.)

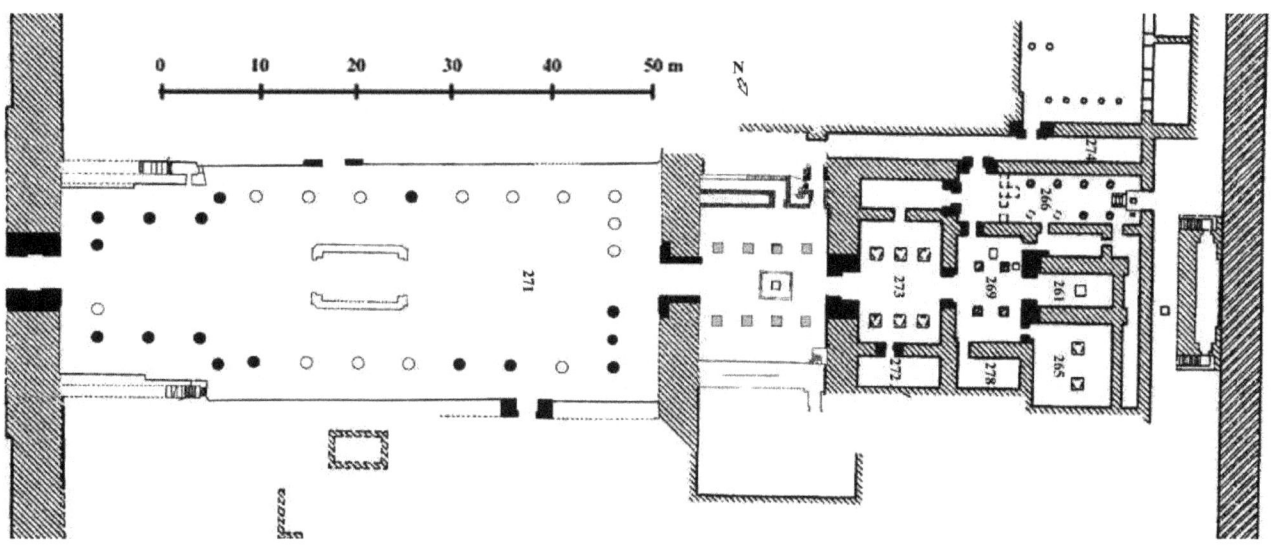

MEROE, Atbara-Khartoum Reach (Sudan)
GPS (DMS): 16.54N 33.44E / Right bank

Postulated Early Amun Temple (Royal City, Area M292-298)

Period: Napatan (and early Meroitic)
Builder(s): Cartouches of the following rulers were found in the area: Senkamanisken, Anlamani, Queen Nalsala, Aspelta, Aramatelqo, Malonaqueñ, Amani-natki-lebte, Karkamani, Amaniastabarqo, Siaspiqo, Talakhamani, and Amanislo.
Orientation: South-north
Measurements: 8.95 x 9.5 metres (interior) [N/A]
Construction materials: Sandstone, red bricks, mud bricks
Preservation status: Over 1m high at the time of Garstang's excavations.

Brief Architectural Description:
Chapel M292 is a small one-room quadrangular building with thick walls. The sole entrance is on the south side and leads into the only room, featuring a podium and four columns. Fragments of columns, roof slabs, blocks inscribed with cartouches of early Napatan kings, and votive objects presumably originating from a temple were unearthed in the vicinity (buildings 293-298).

Select Bibliographical References:
Garstang 1912: 48-51; Hakem 1988: 38-42; Hinkel and Sievertsen 2002: 102-110; Shinnie 1967: 79-80; Shinnie and Anderson 2004: 79-88; Török 1997a: 25-32, 145-168; Zach and Tomandl 2000: 134-135.

Figure 32: Meroe, Postulated Early Amun Temple in Royal City M292-298
(Adapted from Török 1997: Fig. 2.)

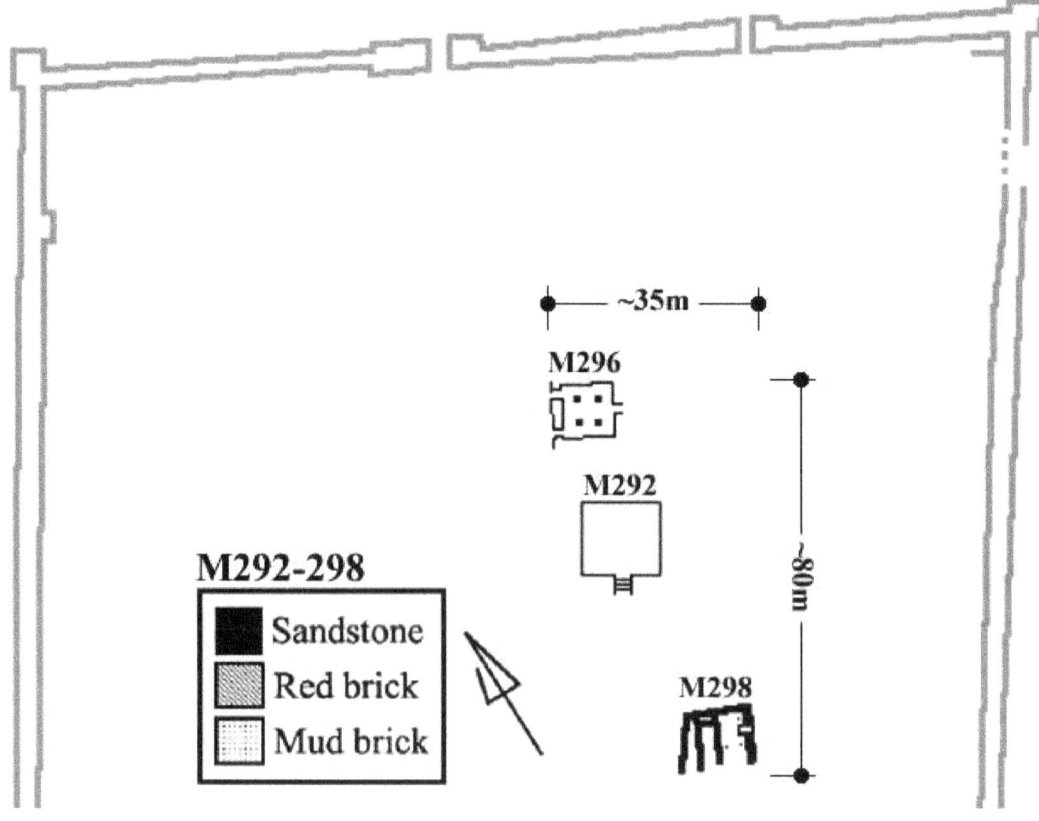

MEROE, Atbara-Khartoum Reach (Sudan)
GPS (DMS): 16.54N 33.44E / Right bank

Isis Temple M600 (previously dedicated to Amun?)

Period:	Meroitic
Builder(s):	Unknown (Stela of Teriteqas found in the 'lower' temple)
Orientation:	East-west
Measurements:	~ 30 x ~12 metres [c]
Construction materials:	Sandstone, red bricks, mud bricks, faience tiles
Preservation status:	N/A

Brief Architectural Description:
Although Garstang's inclusion on the same plan of various construction phases is confusing, the following rooms can be identified: a pyloned forecourt, a hypostyle hall and a central sanctuary with annex rooms behind it and adjoining the south of the hypostyle hall. The 'upper' temple generally follows this plan, but a transverse pronaos and a barque room are added to it.

Select Bibliographical References:
Garstang 1910: 67-69; 1911: 17-19; Hakem 1988: 32-38; Shinnie 1967: 84; Török 1997a: 170-173; Zach and Tomandl 2000: 134.

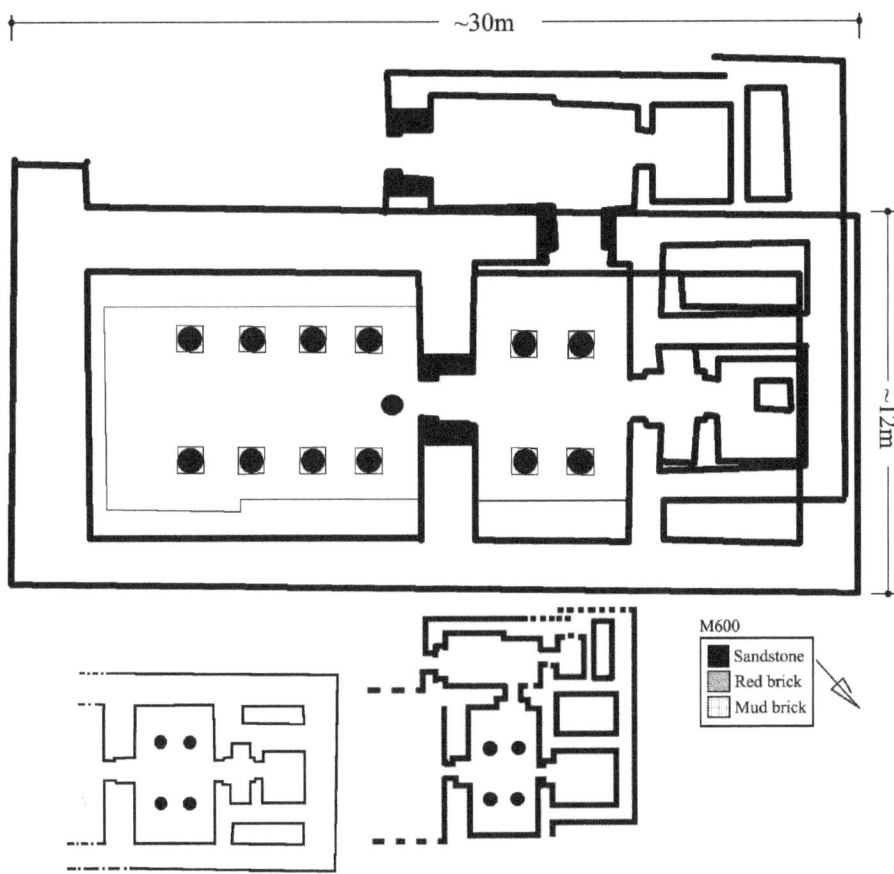

Figure 33: Meroe, Isis Temple M600
(Adapted from Török 1997a: fig. 28 and 1984: 35.)

MEROE, Atbara-Khartoum Reach (Sudan)
GPS (DMS): 16.54N 33.44E / Right bank

Temple M720

Period:	Meroitic
Builder(s):	Unknown
Orientation:	South-north
Measurements:	24 x 13.7 metres [c]
Construction materials:	Sandstone, red bricks, and mud bricks
Preservation status:	Foundation levels.

Brief Architectural Description:
A pylon, now-destroyed, stood at the entrance to this small temple. The first room is a small hall with two columns. The following chamber is a transverse hall without columns that leads into a larger hall where a perambulatory sanctuary is erected within a larger room that did not appear to have been further partitioned. A small altar is present within the perambulatory sanctuary.

Select Bibliographical References:
Bradley 1982: 163-170; 1984a: 421-423; Shinnie 1984: 498-504; Shinnie and Anderson 2004: 20-36; Török 1997a: 178-179; Zach and Tomandl 2000: 135.

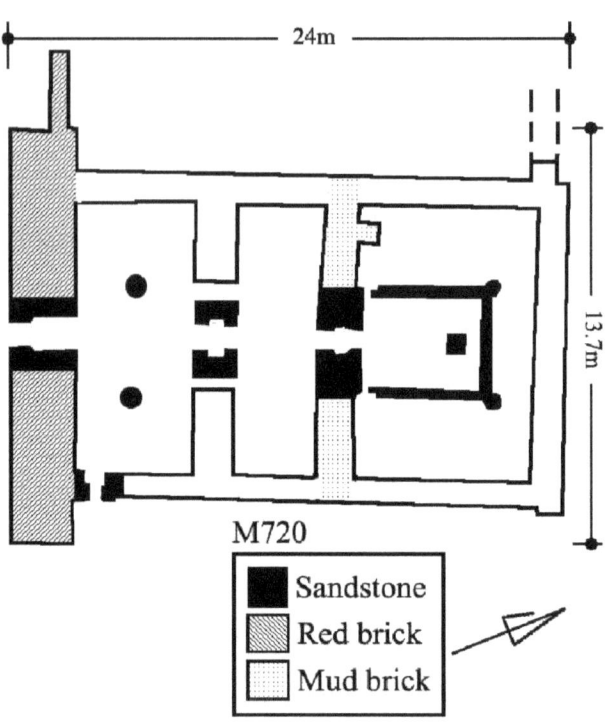

Figure 34: Meroe, Temple M720
(Adapted from Shinnie 1984: 500.)

HAMADAB, Atbara-Khartoum Reach (Sudan)
GPS (DMS): 16.53N 33.41E / Right bank

Temple H1000 (postulated temple to Amun, formerly known as M1000)

Period:	Meroitic
Builder(s):	Unknown (stelae at entrance attributed to Akinidad and Amanirenas (REM 1003 and 1039)
Orientation:	West-east
Measurements:	31 x 16 metres* [M]
Construction materials:	Sandstone, red brick, mud brick
Preservation status:	Over 1 metre high.

Brief Architectural Description:
Two stelae once stood in front of the entrance to this shrine. A thick portal gives access to a long and narrow room with two columns, later engaged, at the far end. In turn, this room gives access to the sanctuary, where an altar is located, as well as to annexes on the north side.

Select Bibliographical References:
Garstang 1916: 1-24; Hakem 1988: 44-47; Lloyd 1970: 196-197; Shinnie 1967: 84-85; Török 1997a: 232-234; Wolf 2002a: 92-104; 2002b: 105-111; 2003: 97-107; Zach and Tomandl 2000: 132.

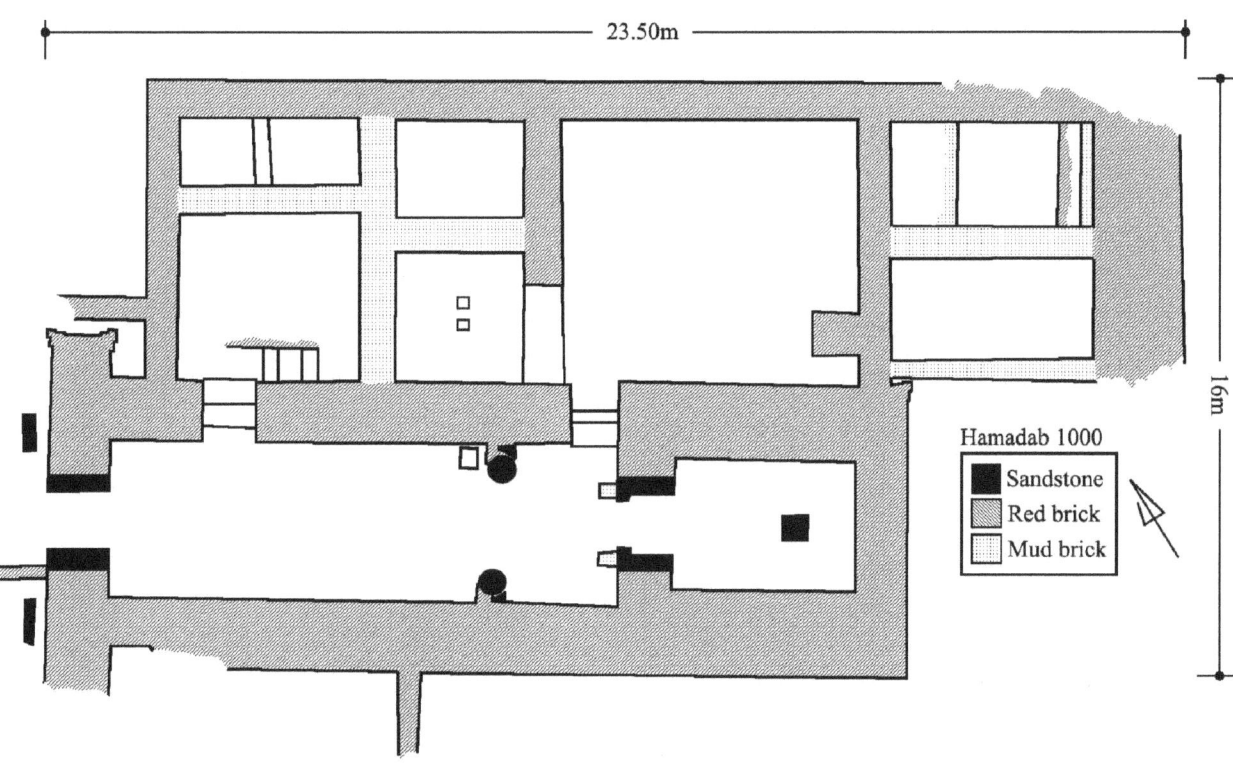

Figure 35: Hamadab, Temple H1000
(Adapted from Török 1997a: fig. 30.)

AWLIB, Atbara-Khartoum Reach (Sudan)
GPS (DMS): 16.52N 33.43E / Right bank

Postulated Temple to Amun (Kôm A)

Period: Napatan/Meroitic (?)
Builder(s):   Unknown
Orientation: East-west
Measurements: 46.27 x 24.23 metres [c]
Construction materials: Sandstone and bricks
Preservation status: Robbed out, height unknown (not fully excavated)

Brief Architectural Description:
The main entrance to this small temple is on the east where the pylon is located. Another small entrance with a hypothesised portico is found on the south side. Although the temple interior has yet to be excavated, a wall at the far end gives the impression of a tripartite division of rooms.

Select Bibliographical References:
Borcowski 2003: 81-84; Hintze 1959: 176; Paner 1997: 137-155; 2003: 3; Zach and Tomandl 2000: 136.

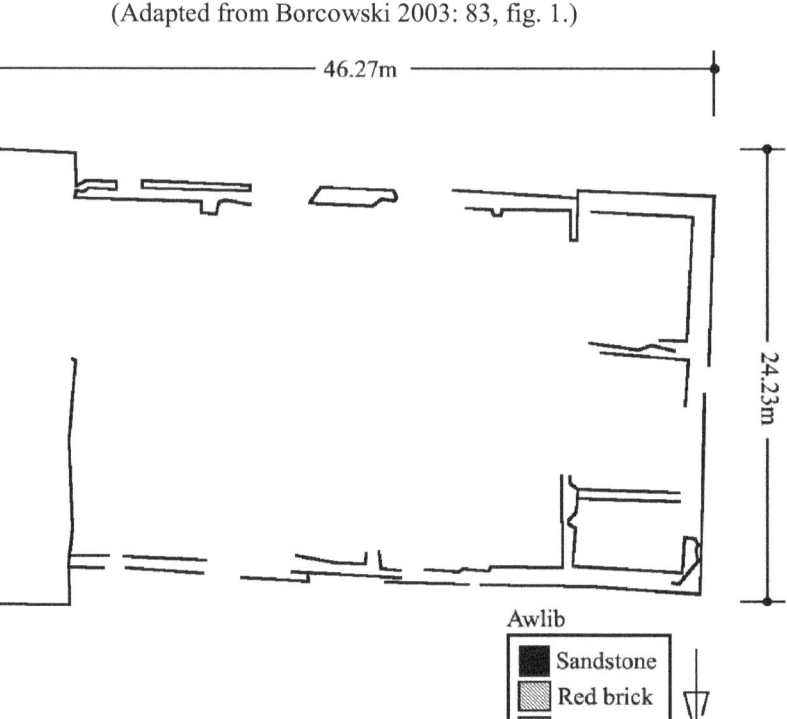

Figure 36: Awlib, Postulated Temple of Amun
(Adapted from Borcowski 2003: 83, fig. 1.)

EL-HASSA, Atbara-Khartoum Reach (Sudan)
GPS (DMS): 16.47.42N 33.36.34E / Right bank
[El-Messa, Meshra el-Hassan, Saiyal Sirag, Deim el-Qarrai, Giblab]

Temple of Amun of Tabakh

Period:	Meroitic
Builder(s):	Amanikhareqerem (?)
Orientation:	East-west, facing the Nile River
Measurements:	Not available
Construction materials:	Red bricks, mud bricks
Preservation status:	Foundations, negative imprints.

Brief Architectural Description:
An avenue of rams and a large pylon fronted the temple. Early in the excavation stages, the following rooms could be distinguished: a hypaethral hall and side rooms with two columns. The hall and the rooms are divided by pillars. A hypostyle hall was expected further into the temple building (Lenoble: personal communication). The final distribution of rooms has yet to be published and remains unavailable at present (Rondot: personal communication).

Select Bibliographical References:
Lenoble and Rondot 2002: 101-111; Rondot and Lenoble 2003: 32.

WAD BAN NAGA, Atbara-Khartoum Reach (Sudan)
GPS (DMS): 16.31N 33.07E / Right bank

Temple WBN300 (dedicated to Amun, Isis, and Hathor (?), South Temple) (Kôm C)

Period:	Meroitic
Builder(s):	Natakamani and Amanitore
Orientation:	West-east
Measurements:	~26.31 (incomplete) x ~21.18 metres [c]
Construction materials:	Bricks
Preservation status:	Destroyed.

Brief Architectural Description:
This now destroyed temple was fronted by a pylon that led to a transverse hypostyle hall with 12 columns (?). Two identical courts *en enfilade* follow and each appears to have given access to side rooms where altars were found (now removed). The sanctuary area is destroyed, but it has been hypothesised that it comprised one central sanctuary (ambulatory shrine?) and two side rooms (accessible from the previous hall).

Select Bibliographical References:
PM VII: 263; Priese 1984a: 347-350; 1984b: 11-29; Zach and Tomandl 2000: 131.

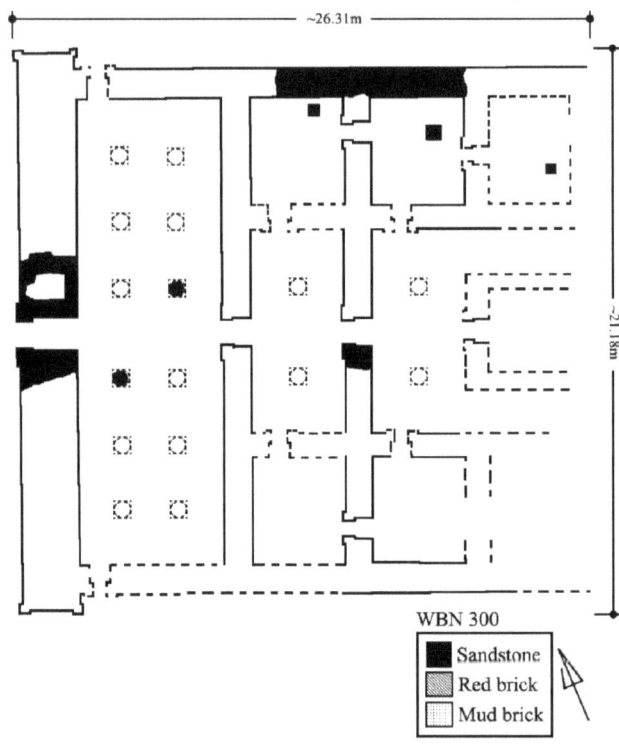

Figure 37: Wad ban Naga, Temple WBN300 (Adapted from Priese 1984b: 17, Abb. 4a.)

WAD BAN NAGA, Atbara-Khartoum Reach (Sudan)
GPS (DMS): 16.31N 33.07E / Right bank

Temple WBN500 (dedicated to Amun (?), East Temple) (Kôm E)

Period:	Meroitic
Builder(s):	Unknown
Orientation:	East-west
Measurements:	Unpublished [N/A]
Construction materials:	Red bricks, sandstone
Preservation status:	Unknown.

Brief Architectural Description:
This small temple comprises a pylon and a hall with eight columns topped with open lotus capitals. It opens to two transverse column-less halls and ends in a triple sanctuary.

Select Bibliographical References:
Hakem 1988: 322-326; PM VII: 263; Priese 1984a: 11-29; 1984b: 347-350; Vercoutter 1962b: 263-299.

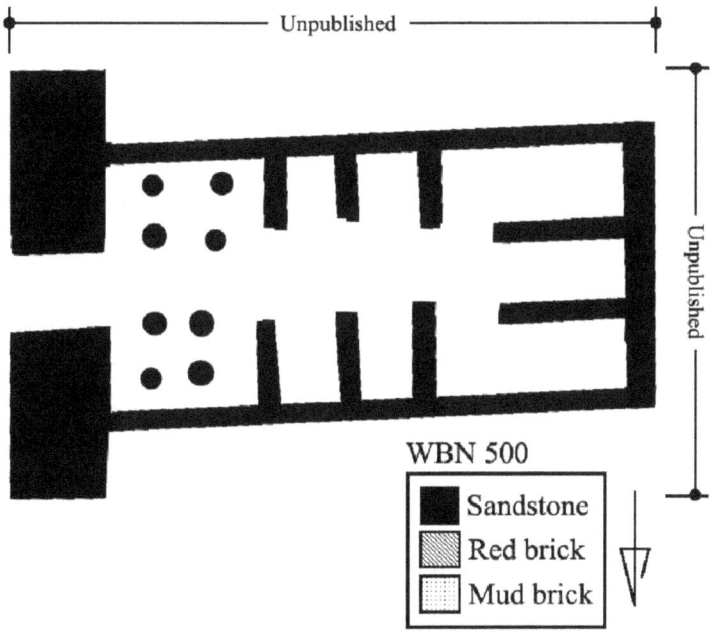

Figure 38: Wad ban Naga, Temple WBN500
(Adapted from Vercoutter 1962b: 271, p. 2.)

ALEM, Butana (Sudan)
GPS (DMS): 16.59N 33.55E / Right bank

Meroitic Temple

Period: Meroitic
Builder(s):   Unknown
Orientation: East-west
Measurements: 21.65 x 5.10 metres [M]
Construction materials: Red brick, sandstone, ferricrete
Preservation status: Foundation levels.

Brief Architectural Description:
Very little information is available regarding this building. The temple is accessed by a ramp that broadens more than halfway up. There are two rooms *en enfilade*; the last one contains a small yellow sandstone altar.

Select Bibliographical References:
Addison and Dunham 1922; Hinkel 1985: 163-180; Hintze 1959: 178; Zach and Tomandl 2000: 136.

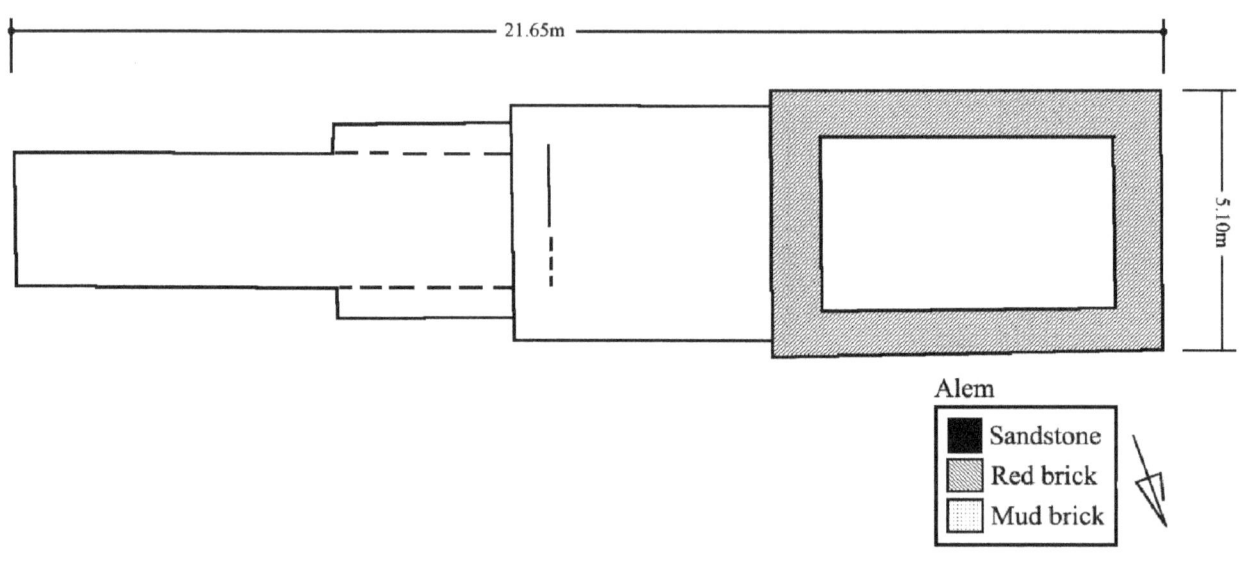

Figure 39: Alem, Meroitic Temple
(Adapted from Hinkel 1985: fig. 3.)

DUANIB, Butana (Sudan)
GPS (DMS): 16.31N 33.22E / Right bank
[Wadi el-Banat, Wadi e Temied]

Temple I, Postulated Temple to Amun

Period:	Meroitic
Builder(s):	Natakamani
Orientation:	N/A
Measurements:	6.11 x 4.80 metres [?]
Construction materials:	Stone
Preservation status:	Destroyed.

Brief Architectural Description:
Single room temple without a pylon or columns. Unfortunately, only a plan of the site is available in the Hintze Archives (Archiv der Berlin-Brandenburgischen Akademie der Wissenschaften) (Wenig: personal communication).

Select Bibliographical References:
Hakem 1988: 321; Hintze 1959: 176; PM VII: 262; Zach and Tomandl 2000: 143-144.

MUSAWWARAT ES-SUFRA, Butana (Sudan)
GPS (DMS): 16.25N 33.22E

Temple IA 100 (Central Temple, Temple 100)

Period:	Meroitic
Builder(s):	Arnekhamani
Orientation:	East-west
Measurements:	14 x 11 metres [M]
Construction materials:	Sandstone
Preservation status:	Over 2 meters high.

Brief Architectural Description:
The central temple of the Great Enclosure has a unique architectural plan. It is located on a platform and surrounded by several small rooms. The temple is also surrounded by a peristyle colonnade that had a second row of columns on the east side. The main entrance is located beyond this double set of columns and there is a second doorway on the north side. It has been concluded that this little room was lit by four windows. Four columns are erected inside it. A large niched shrine is carved in the west wall, while a smaller one is carved in the south wall.

Select Bibliographical References:
Hakem 1988: 214-219; PM VII: 264-265; Shinnie 1967: 92-94; Török 1997b: 399-400; Welsby 1996: 145-146; Wenig 2001: 71-86; Zach and Tomandl 2000: 138.

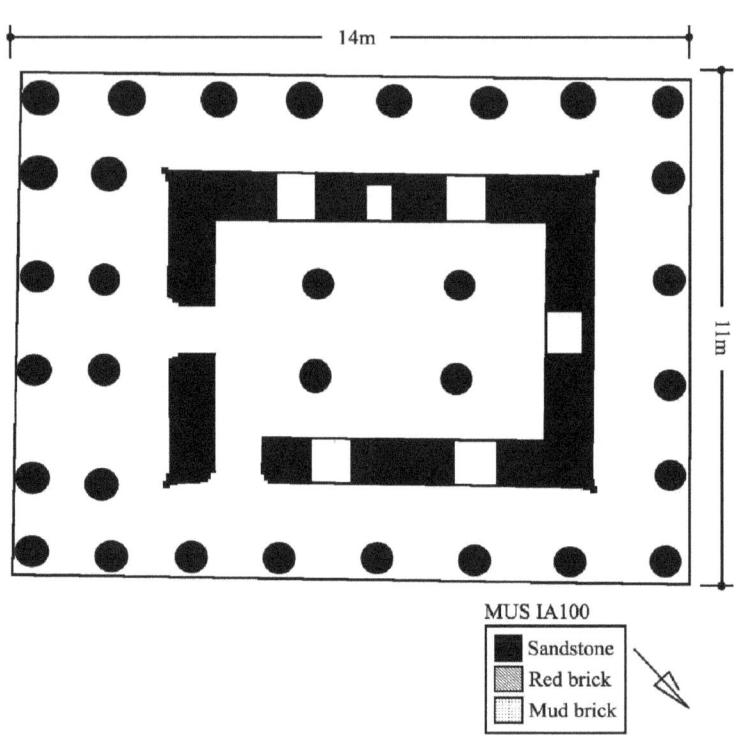

Figure 40: Musawwarat es-Sufra, Temple IA 100
(Adapted from Wenig 2001: 77, 7.)

UMM SODA, Butana (Sudan)
GPS (DMS): 16.18.24N 34.19.40E
[Um Usuda]

Postulated Temple

Period: Meroitic

Brief Architectural Description
N/A

Select Bibliographical References:
Crowfoot 1911: 20-24; Griffith 1911: 69; Hakem 1988: 326-327; Hofmann and Tomandl 1986: 87-90; PM VII: 272; Shinnie 1967: 95-96.

NAGA, Butana (Sudan)
GPS (DMS): 16.16N 33.18E / Right bank (desert)
[Wadi Awateb]

Temple N100, Temple of Amun of Tolkte (Lepsius' Temple c-d)

Period:	Meroitic
Builder(s):	Natakamani and Amanitore (and Prince Arkhamani)
Orientation:	West-east, in the desert 40 km away from the Nile
Measurements:	100 x 30 metres (33x 30 metres without the ramp) [c]
Construction materials:	Sandstone, red bricks, mud bricks
Preservation status:	Standing pylon gateway, over 1m high.

Brief Architectural Description:
The temple is located on a platform accessed by a principal ramp. The avenue displays rams and a kiosk. The main temple pylon is the entrance to the temple proper, and leads to a transverse hypostyle hall. The next two rooms are smaller, both have the same width, and neither has columns. The second of these halls acts as a pronaos that leads into a sanctuary. Two side doors give access to elongated chambers, including an altar/dais room, situated between these two rooms and the exterior wall of the temple. These narrow side chambers are connected to smaller rooms located beside the sanctuary. The northern room gives access to a transverse room behind the sanctuary. A lone ram sits at the back, outside the temple proper, in a contra-temple.

Select Bibliographical References:
Kroeper and Krzyżaniak 1998: 203-216; Kroeper and Wildung 2002: 135-140; LD I: 143-145; PM VII 267-272; REM: 0023-0038; Wildung 1998: 183-187; 1999.

Figure 41: Naga, Temple N100
(Adapted from Kroeper and Wildung 2002: 135.)

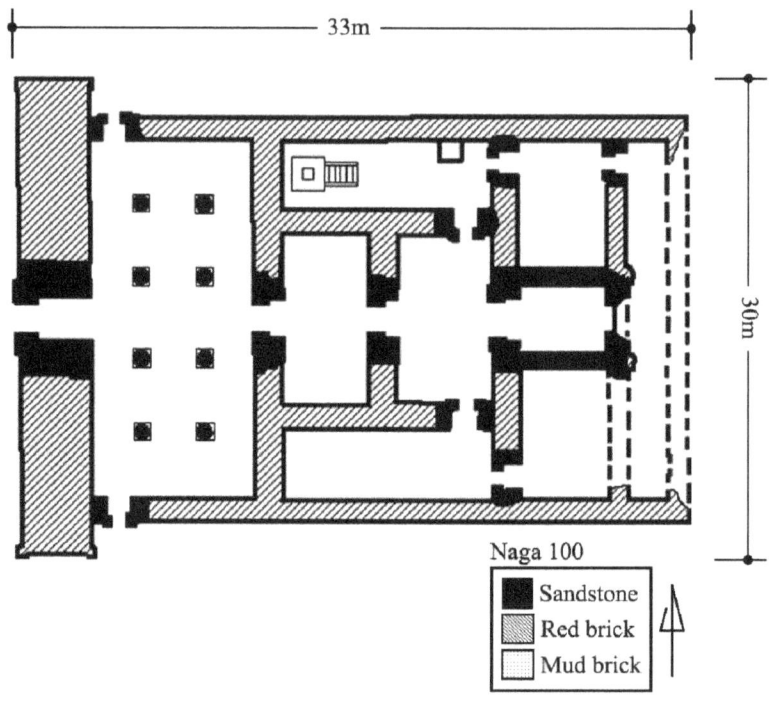

NAGA, Butana (Sudan)

GPS (DMS): 16.16N 33.18E / Right bank (desert)
[Wadi Awateb]

Temple N500, Temple of Amun (with guest cults?) (Lepsius' Temple f)

Period: Meroitic
Builder(s): Queen Shanakdakhete
Orientation: South-north, at the foot of Gebel Naga
Measurements: 16.34 x ~9.81 metres [M]
Construction materials: Sandstone
Preservation status: Approximately 2 m high.

Brief Architectural Description:
Although built at the foot of Gebel Naga, this temple is a free-standing structure. A small portico with four columns and screens gives access to a single room where there are four columns and a small altar. A niche is carved in the back wall.

Select Bibliographical References:
Hakem 1988: 310-311; Hinkel 1991: fig. 7; Hintze 1959: 184-185; Hofmann, Tomandl, and Zach 1985: 27-35; LD: Ab1, Bld. 145; PM VII: 271; Tomandl and Zach 2000: 139-143; Török 1997a: 149-150; Wildung 1999: 74; Zach 1999: 685-699.

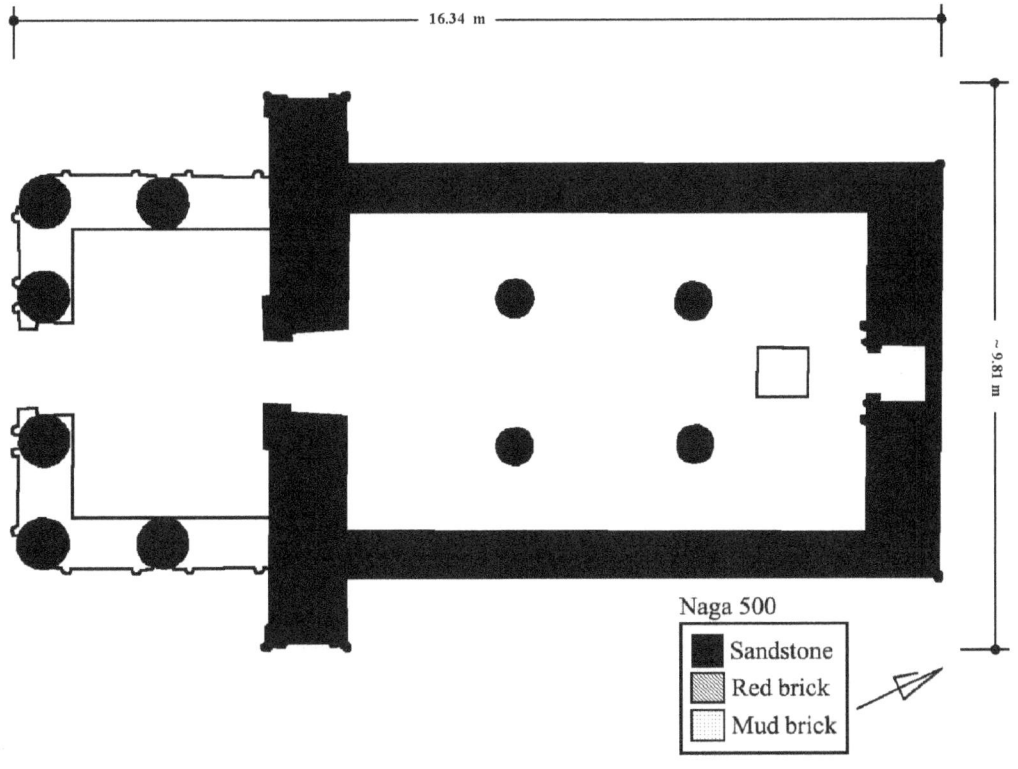

Figure 42: Naga, Temple N500
(Adapted from Hinkel 1991: fig. 7.)

SOBA EAST, Gezira (Sudan)
GPS (DMS): 15.40N 32.32E / Right bank of the Blue Nile

Postulated Temple

Period: Napatan / Meroitic

Brief Architectural Description
N/A

Select Bibliographical References:
Hakem 1988: 302-303; Hofmann 1981; Orlando 2003: 85-88; PM VII: 276; REM 0001; Shinnie 1967: 97; Welsby 1983; 1984; Welsby and Daniels 1991; Wenig 1999: 678-684.

CHAPTER 3. IDENTIFICATION OF AMUN TEMPLES IN NUBIA

INTRODUCTION

Scholars have identified—with varying degrees of certitude—numerous temples in which Amun was thought to have been worshipped. These sacred buildings were presented in the previous chapter. However, in order to undertake a proper typological study of the architectural plan of these temples, they must be identified with certainty. Therefore, a critical review of the study corpus is necessary.

Within the present study, the positive identification of an Amun temple is based on the following two criteria: the presence of monumental ram statues (or criosphinxes)—the avatar of Amun—and/or the identification of Amun as the principal deity by means of an inscription discovered in a secure archaeological context. This epigraphic evidence, for example, can be obtained from the texts and decorative reliefs on walls, on a stela erected within the temple itself or at the entrance, or, in the case of a destroyed temple, from foundation deposit plaques. Additional historical documents can also be used provided that the archaeological site to which they refer can be correctly identified.

THE DIFFICULTIES OF IDENTIFICATION

Amongst all the studied sacred buildings, the Egyptian and Napatan temples are the most readily identified. Most having been constructed of stone, these temples have survived much better the ravages of time. Formal temple decoration was carved directly into the stone, in bas-relief or *en creux*, and then painted. Although the colours have faded under the intense sunlight or were washed away by the annual rains, the carved reliefs still remain today. New Kingdom and Napatan royal inscriptions and stelae found within the temple precincts were not only better preserved, they were, most importantly, written in a language that was deciphered and is now well understood.

In contrast, the walls of Meroitic temples were generally constructed with red bricks to form a casing around a mud brick core; the door jambs and the columns were the rare features made of poor-quality Nubian sandstone. The extremely poor state of preservation of Meroitic buildings is due in part to the climate and the environment: the heavy rains are much more frequent in central Sudan than they are in southern Egypt (Adams 1984: 277) and these construction materials, which reflect the available natural resources in the south, do not fare well in such climatic conditions. Additionally, red bricks and mud bricks—the cheap materials commonly used for the great architectural commissions of Meroitic rulers—provide easily accessible construction materials and fertilisers for modern villagers today. The ancient brick buildings of the Sudan—like those of Egypt—have suffered from these "recycling" activities. In some parts of the country, the damage is considerable; many of the temples have been robbed down to their foundations, and all that remains are negative impressions.

The nature of brick as a construction material dictates the methods of decoration to be employed. Unlike walls constructed of sandstone blocks, those of bricks were not carved. The walls were first covered with a thick mud plaster, then whitewashed with lime, and finally colourfully painted with text, decorative scenes, and motifs. Upon such fragile wall decorations, the heavy annual rains were fatal. Not only did the paint wash away, the mud plaster crumbled off the wall or turned into a puddle of mud on the floor.

Specimens of such rare temple decorations have been found at Meroe (Bradley 1984a: 421-423; 2003: 66-70), Dangeil (Anderson and Ahmed 2006b), and el-Hassa (Lenoble: personal communication) among other sites. In general, these painted mud plaster fragments were discovered in a chaotic heap and could only be partially reconstructed due to the lack of corresponding pieces. Fortunately, remains of the mud plaster decoration of the pronaos at Dangeil had fallen as a large chunk of plaster, which cracked as it hit the sandstone floor but remained in a coherent unit. Thus it was possible—although painstakingly so because several layers of mud had fused the fragments together during the annual rains—for the author to reassemble the fragments that joined to reconstruct the design. The newly assembled fragments showed parts of an inscription and sections of a scene were preserved; however, they did not reveal new information about the temple, *per se*. In the inscription, the nine hieroglyphs and word dividers (three horizontal dots) are the same as the inscribed scene on the first gate at Naga (REM 0026) (Anderson and Ahmed 2006b: 3) and the scene represents the lotus headdress of a fertility deity.

Inscriptions and decorations painted on Meroitic brick temple walls are therefore rare and archaeologists must rely on monuments carved in hard ferricrete sandstone, regular but softer Nubian sandstone, or granite, which were generally used for ram statues, altars, stelae, and, occasionally, for column drums. Even when some inscriptions are preserved, archaeologists face the same problem of the still undeciphered Meroitic language, which makes the identification of the deity difficult.

Although over one thousand inscriptions in Meroitic hieroglyphs or cursive Meroitic script have been found (see Leclant *et al.* 2000, *Répertoire d'épigraphie méroïtique*), Meroitic studies are heavily dependant on archaeological excavations and comparative analyses of the discovered materials simply because our knowledge of this ancient language is still too limited. Until

Meroitic is deciphered, most of these inscriptions and stelae cannot be used by scholars to further their understanding of this civilisation. The name of the god Amun (Amani) is one of the few Meroitic words identifiable in textual documents. However, in most cases, because the rest of the sentence (let alone the entire text) in which the name of Amun appears is generally obscure, it is of little help.

The ram or criosphinx statue, even without an accompanying dedication, is, however, the positive and secure identification of the god Amun as the honoured deity of a temple. The Amun ram (*ovis platyra aegyptiaca*) is distinguished from other species of rams by the curved horns around the ears, although the twisted horizontal horns of *ovis longipes palaeoaegyptiaca* are a feature of Amun Gematon. These curved horns of Amun were part of the king's paraphernalia from the New Kingdom onwards; they were symbols of divinity associated with the cult of the deified king (Török 1987: 45) and of the king's union with Amun (Bell 1997: 170), because the ruler had been chosen by Amun (Török 1987: 46). Such ram statues and criosphinges have only been found in relation to buildings dedicated to Amun. The absence of the ram statue, however, does not signify that the temple is not dedicated to Amun. An Amun temple without ram or criosphinx statues likely served a different cultic purpose or function, or indicated that Amun was worshipped along with other deities, Egyptian or Nubian, who were equally important.

Furthermore, Meroitic temples have not survived the millennia very well because, chronologically speaking, they could not have been extensively restored by later generations of rulers as was the case with earlier Egyptian temples.

IDENTIFICATION OF AMUN TEMPLES

Temples Identified by Inscriptions and Rams
The well-known Amun temples at Gebel Barkal (B500), Meroe (M260), Naga (N100), Kawa (Temple T), and Soleb have all been identified with certainty by artefacts, inscriptions on the temple walls, and various royal documents[7] as well as by the pairs of ram statues lining the dromos of the temple. The granite rams in front of the Great Temple of Amun at Gebel Barkal were brought from the Temple of Amun and Nebmaatrē at Soleb. Two extremely weatherworn rams were left *in situ* at Soleb (Schiff-Giorgini *et al.* 2002: 19), and several curved horns fragments were found scattered on the site and in the old Schiff-Giorgini storerooms.[8] Similarly, one pair of granite rams was left *in situ* at Kawa (Temple T), while the second pair was divided and relocated: one ram is now in the British Museum (EA 1779), while the other is in the National Museum in Khartoum. Four of the original six black ferricrete sandstone rams at Meroe are still located in front of the pylon of M260 (Lepsius 1849, pl. 132; see also Grzymski 2003: 6). Temple N100 at Naga boasts the processional avenue with the most ram sculptures currently extant in Nubia. There are 12 rams *couchant* placed on high pedestals; three pairs are located in front of the kiosk, while the remaining three pairs are situated behind it.

Temples Identified by an Inscription
The temples at Aksha, Amara East, Amara West, Dabod, Doukki Gel, Gebel Barkal (B700), Kawa (Temples A and B), Naga (N500), Sai Island (Temple A), and Sanam have all been identified as temples dedicated to Amun by inscriptions found either on the remaining upstanding walls of the temple, artefacts found on site[9] or, in the case of destroyed buildings, in plaques discovered in the foundation deposits.

Occasionally, the evidence for the identification of a temple has since been destroyed and must be based on travelogues of early explorers. This is partly the case for temple B700 at Gebel Barkal. As observed by Frédéric Cailliaud's during his travels (1819-1822), the temple pylon—which is now completely destroyed—showed inscribed reliefs dedicating the temple to Amun-Rē (Reisner 1918: 104). At the present time, the only evidence of the dedication to Amun-Rē is the short inscription on the granite altar found in the temple, in room 703 (Reisner 1918: 104-105).

The Meroitic temple at Amara East has never been excavated and only Griffith studied the inscriptions on the sandstone columns before the temple disappeared under the sands or was destroyed between 1860 and 1905. The study of the inscriptions, which are now included in the *Répertoire d'épigraphie méroïtique* (REM 0084, 0144-0150) demonstrates that the temple was built by King Natakamani, Queen Amanitore, and Prince Sherkarer, and that it was dedicated to Amun. Additionally, the dedication to Amun can be further demonstrated by the fact that these inscriptions and reliefs are identical to those of the Temple of Amun (N100) at Naga.

In the case of destroyed temples, possible *in situ* epigraphic identification often comes from foundation

---

[7] Inscriptions cannot be mentioned individually here; however, note that these can be found in the following publications: ***Les cultes d'Amon hors de Thèbes*** (Guermeur 2005), which presents the inscriptions for the identification of Amun temples dated to the New Kingdom and the Napatan Period; the *Répertoire d'épigraphie méroïtique* (Leclant *et al.* 2000) in which Meroitic inscriptions are documented, and ***Fontes Historiae Nubiorum*** (Eide *et al.* 1994-1998), which includes both Napatan and Meroitic inscriptions.

[8] I am indebted to Dr Hourig Sourouzian who, in December 2000, was kind enough to allow me to join her on a research trip to Soleb, where we explored the old Schiff-Giorgini storerooms and recovered several fragments of curled ram horns mentioned above.

[9] The seven statues discovered in the Kerma/Doukki Gel *cachette* confirmed both the identity of the god worshipped in the temples as well as the ancient Egyptian name of the site (Bonnet and Valbelle 2005: 11). See comments below, p. 61ff.

deposits. As an example, the New Kingdom temple on Sai Island (Temple A) was identified as a sacred building to Amun by the foundation deposits, on which the name of the god had not been mutilated during the Amarna period, as had the inscriptions and figures on the walls (Vercoutter 1974: 32). Likewise, the dilapidated temple at Sanam, across the river from Gebel Barkal, was also identified thanks to the foundation deposits (Griffith 1922: 82) and remnants of the dedication on a wall of the first court (PM VII: 199).

The small temple erected at the foot of Gebel Naga (N500) is dedicated to the ram-headed Amun, but he was not the sole deity worshipped in this building (Wolf 2006: 257; Zach and Tomandl 2000: 139-143; Zach: personal communication). Although Shanakdakhete is shown adoring Amun sitting on a throne with Mut behind him on the south wall (east end), it was impossible to identify the other deities in the other scenes. The temple, the oldest at Naga, is damaged and several figures have lost their heads and identifiable headgear. It has been suggested that Amun shared his lodgings with Apedemak, either as a guest or co-resident. Additionally, Zach has put forward the hypothesis of a double cult of Amun as part of the Theban Triad and the divine couple Apedemak and Amesemi. One of the figures might also be a deified predecessor of Shanakdakhete (Zach: personal communication).

Temples Identified by Ram Statues
During the 2003 excavation season at Dangeil, three sandstone fragments representing ram eyes painted in red were found in front of the temple's portico. This area, which is littered with coloured plaster fragments and large quantities of sandstone and red brick debris, revealed rectangular platforms that have been identified as the pedestals for the ram statues. Amongst the rubble were discovered a few sandstone fragments carved with a pattern of overlapping ovals (much like fish scales), the treatment of the fleece found on the rams at el-Hassa and Soba. This same scale-like pattern is also found drawn in red on yellow-painted plaster.

The newly discovered Amun temple at el-Hassa currently has one ram *in situ*, fallen off its pedestal in front of the temple. Another ram had been discovered in 1975 during the digging of a canal; however, it disappeared in 2000. The Soba ram, now in Khartoum, is said to have been removed from el-Hassa (see below). In total, three rams are associated with el-Hassa.

Gebel Barkal B800, located west of the Great Temple of Amun (B500), appears to have been built by Kashta, at the time when the New Kingdom temple of Amun (core of B500) had fallen in ruins (Kendall 1992a: 141). Reisner discovered two uninscribed rams of red sandstone in front of B800, buried under a late Meroitic mud brick structure in front of the temple (1931: 80). Reisner did not complete the excavation in this area, and the structure in front of the temple (labelled B850), under which the statues were found, remains unpublished to this day (Kendall 1992a: 141). Although, the rams are associated with B800-First, they are generally mentioned in reference to B850.

Ram God without a Temple
The archaeological sites of Soba and Umm Soda have one of the two prerequisite criteria indicating the presence of an Amun temple: the ram statue. Explorers and archaeologists have described and researched these statues and their inscription; however, the temples dedicated to Amun have yet to be located and unearthed at both Soba and Umm Soda.

According to Griffith (1911: 52-53), the presence of the ram statue discovered at Soba indicated that an Amun temple had once been erected on this site. Presently, however, several scholars argue that this lone ram had been transported there from el-Hassa (Wenig 1999; Orlando 2003: 86-87). Indeed, stylistically, the el-Hassa and Soba rams share numerous physical characteristics, notably the rendering of the fleece. Additionally, the inscriptions found on the base of both ram statues suggest that they were commissioned by the same king. The cartouche on the base of the now lost el-Hassa ram (REM 1151) was reinterpreted by Wenig (1999) as *Mḫrekerem*, the name also found on the famous Soba ram (REM 0001).

The above evidence strongly suggests that indeed the rams were commissioned by the same ruler and, because of their artistic similarities, flanked the processional avenue of the same temple. During recent excavations at el-Hassa, the French mission located the large Meroitic temple erected in honour of Amun and have discovered a third ram statue, fallen off its rectangular brick base in front of the pylon. It bore the same inscription and was carved with the same features as the previously mentioned rams (Rondot and Lenoble 2003). El-Hassa is believed to be the home of the Soba ram.

This belief now encourages scholars to abandon the idea of an Amun temple at Soba, forgetting that its presence so far south has yet to be explained. In the author's opinion, the possibility of finding an Amun temple at Soba remains probable. It must not be forgotten that statues of considerable size have previously been dragged across the desert to adorn a later temple dedicated to the same god. The rams and lions at Soleb, originally part of the processional avenue of the jubilee temple of Amenhotep III, were transported to Gebel Barkal by King Amanislo and installed in front of the Great Temple of Amun of Napata. With such a precedent, the removal of a ram from el-Hassa and its relocation at Soba to decorate a later temple to Amun becomes the most logical explanation for its presence so far south.

Although the excavations at Soba have concentrated on the Christian remains, there is some evidence of Napatan and Meroitic occupation on the site, some of which has been excavated (Welsby 1999: 663-677). A recently discovered glass lion's head dated to the Meroitic period, a sphinx, and a relief of the goddess Hathor have been excavated. In addition to Shinnie's Napatan scarabs and "a few pre-Christian antiquities," these artefacts add considerable weight to the hypothesis suggesting that there is an as yet undiscovered Amun temple at Soba (Welsby and Daniels 1991: 6). Building G, a structure presumably religious in nature, was discovered west of an extensive cemetery (Welsby 1998: 275). The second construction phase of Building G shares similarities with Meroitic temples, but its exact function could not be determined (Welsby 1998: 277).

The probability of discovering an Amun temple at Umm Soda is even greater than at Soba. In 1907, Crowfoot visited the site, where he observed much evidence of Meroitic occupation: circular water reservoirs (*hafirs*) of various sizes, several stone statues, and a Meroitic inscription. Although the statues were extremely weather-worn, their general shape and some details permitted their identification as seven lions and three rams *couchant*.[10] Two of these rams were much smaller in scale than the third one (Crowfoot 1911: 28; Hofmann and Tomandl 1986: 89).

The presence of *hafirs*, a few graves (Hakem 1988: 327), the Meroitic inscription, and the statues would indicate a substantial Meroitic site, with, at the very least, one temple dedicated to Amun and Apedemak—if not two temples, one for each god. Unfortunately, the stela does not reveal the name of any deity and the ruins of the temple(s) have yet to be discovered. However, once again, it is quite probable that a temple dedicated to Amun existed at Umm Soda. Only further excavations can provide scholars with the long-awaited answers.

IDENTIFICATION OF ANCIENT PNUBS

A Tale of Two Cities
Various coronation stelae of the Kushite kings listed the site of Pnubs as one of the stations of the coronation journey undertaken by the new Kushite ruler after his accession to the throne. The inscriptions were consistent; they all listed the Great Temple of Amun of Napata, the Temple of Amun Gematon, and the Temple of Amun of Pnubs. The fourth temple, the Temple of Amun, Bull of Nubia, appeared in early stelae but was excluded from the time of Harsiotef onwards. Indeed, Harsiotef (Annals of Year 35) and Nastasen (Stela of Year 8) introduced the Temple of Bastet of Tare instead (FHN II: 443, FHN II 483; Hakem 1988: 103). The Temple of Amun of Napata was identified by Reisner as B500 at Gebel Barkal (Reisner 1918: 99), the Temple of Amun, Bull of Nubia as the ruins at Sanam by Griffith (1922: 18), and the Temple of Amun Gematon as the large temple built by Taharqo at Kawa (Temple T) by Macadam (1955: 61). These three temples were all identified by inscriptions and written materials found during the excavations.

Until recently, two cities were at the centre of the discussion regarding the location of the ancient city of Pnubs: Tabo on Argo Island and Kerma. It was a study of the military invasion mentioned on the stela of Psammetichus II that allowed scholars like Yoyotte and Sauneron to deduce that the site of Pnubs was located south of the Third Cataract, but north of Kawa on the east bank of the Nile, in the vicinity of Kerma/Argo Island. (1952: 163-169). However, the exact location of the site had yet to be determined. Macadam suggested Argo Island as the location of ancient Pnubs (1949: xiv-xv, 60 §E, note 99). Argo Island does indeed lie south of the Third Cataract and north of Kawa, and the site becomes an island only during the inundation. Until the excavation of the site of Tabo under the directorship of Charles Maystre of the Université de Genève, the matter was mere speculation. A large temple structure—albeit extremely ruinous—was unearthed and circumstantial evidence suggested that Amun was worshipped on this island, in this temple: a statue fragment of the sun disc and double feathers of the god's crown, a small amulet in the shape of a round-topped stela depicting the Theban Triad, several amulets in the shape of a criosphinx, a ram's head, and a feathered sun disc (Jacquet-Gordon *et al.* 1969: 111). Additionally, what architectural plan could be made out amongst the ruins of the temple resembled that of the coronation temples of Taharqo at Kawa and Sanam. Although the worship of Amun at Tabo appears likely, the epigraphic evidence identifying the site as Pnubs is almost nil (Bonnet and Valbelle 2000: 1118-1119). The only mention of Amun of Pnubs came from a fragment of an inscription, of which only one-third remained, and the name Pnubs was extrapolated from the presence of a single letter *b* (Jacquet-Gordon *et al.* 1969: 111; Bonnet and Valbelle 2000: 1118). Yet, from that moment onwards, the large temple on site was referred to as the Temple of Amun of Pnubs, even though the evidence was scanty at best.

Over twenty-five years ago, the burial of Penimen, a *w'b* priest of Amun of Pnubs, was found at Kerma (Bonnet and Valbelle 1980). However, because the bronze bowl on which the dedication had been inscribed was an object that could have travelled and the location of the burial at Kerma did not indicate that the temple itself was located on site, the idea that Pnubs could be identified with Kerma was not pressed by the excavators (Bonnet and Valbelle 1980; 2000: 1117). Yet other scholars, notably Wolf in his unpublished Ph.D. thesis (1990) (as cited in Bonnet and Valbelle 2000: 1119) and Török (1997b: 140), suggested that Pnubs should actually be equated with the long-famed site of Kerma. As with Tabo, the site

---
[10] Crowfoot reports seeing three ram statues (1911: 23), but Hakem mentions four of them (1988: 327).

of Kerma is located south of the Third Cataract and north of Kawa. Moreover, unlike the temporary island of Argo, the location is truly on the east bank. With Tabo and Kerma in close proximity, it is possible to substitute one for the other in the calculation of the northernmost coronation journey stations.

The recent discovery and excavation of the religious ruins of Doukki Gel, approximately 1 km north of the Western *Deffufa* at Kerma, has laid the discussion to rest. The ancient city of Pnubs is to be equated with Kerma, specifically with the site of Doukki Gel. In the past few years, numerous temples dated to the New Kingdom as well as the Napatan and Meroitic periods were discovered at Doukki Gel. The superimposition of numerous architectural remains and associated levels are extremely complex (Bonnet and Valbelle 2005: 27), but the epigraphic evidence is clear.

Numerous inscriptions revealed that a number of the sacred buildings erected on site from the early Eighteenth Dynasty onwards were dedicated to Amun. Traces of the frenzied Amarna destruction of the name of Amun are visible on numerous blocks. Several private Eighteenth Dynasty monuments also attest to the presence of Amun of Pnubs on site (Valbelle 2003: 210). Later Napatan and Meroitic epigraphic evidence also attests to the presence of Amun of Pnubs within the temples (Valbelle 2003: 210). Quantities of blocks dismantled from the Napatan and Meroitic temples, inscribed with the name "Amun of Pnubs," literally litter the site.

The identity of the site was confirmed in January 2003, with the discovery of seven statues of Twenty-fifth Dynasty and Napatan kings (Taharqo, Tanwetamani, Senkamanisken, Anlamani, and Aspelta) inside a *cachette* in the western temple. Each statue was inscribed on the base or the back pillar with the king's royal titulary and the epithet "Beloved of Amun of Pnubs" (*mry 'Imn n p3-nbs*) or "Beloved of Amun-Rē residing in Pnubs" (*mry 'Imn-Rᶜ ḥry ib p3-nbs*) (Valbelle 2003: 199). This great discovery gave a sensation of déjà-vu because, in 1916, Reisner found similar statues in the Gebel Barkal cache and each of them also bore the king's titulary and the epithet "Beloved of Amun of Napata, Lord of the Thrones of the Two Lands" (Reisner 1917: 216-217; cf. Valbelle 2003: 199). The inscriptions on these statues not only confirmed the identity of the chief deity worshipped in the numerous temples, they also confirmed the name given to this locality by the ancient Egyptians: Pnubs (Bonnet and Valbelle 2005: 11).

The location of ancient Pnubs is now finally resolved, but the large temple at Tabo remains to this day an enigma. Jacquet-Gordon, who believes the epigraphic evidence at Doukki Gel does not adequately support the identification of that site as ancient Pnubs, still favours Tabo (Jacquet-Gordon: personal communication).

INCONCLUSIVE IDENTIFICATION OF TEMPLE OR SITE

The temples that have not met the criteria to be positively identified as Amun temples are listed below in the order they are found in the Gazetteer (from north to south). A few words were thought necessary to explain why they had not been definitely identified.

Amada
Although Amun is clearly present in the decoration programme of the temple at Amada, inscriptions never refer to Amun as resident deity (Dewachter 1987: 190). According to Dewachter, Amun is present in the temple decoration simply because of his importance as dynastic god (1987: 190-191). Although early scholars who studied the temple believed it to be dedicated to Amun as well as Rē-Horakhty,[11] it can be argued that Amun is not the subject of any cult at Amada.

Aniba
In the temple of Re-Horakhty at Amada, there is a wall inscription in Chamber J that refers to Amun as "Lord of the Thrones of the Two Lands, Great God who Resides in Miam" (*imn nb nswt t3wy nṯr ᶜ3 ḥry ib Miᶜm*) (Barguet *et al.* 1967: 31).[12] This is the only mention of Amun of Miam and, at Aniba itself, a temple to this god has yet to be discovered.

Qasr Ibrim
Temple 1, a Post-Meroitic temple built in the East Peninsula, was excavated in 1964 and the ruins of the west wall revealed re-used inscribed blocks dating to the New Kingdom (Ramses IV). Plumley identified these as coming from an Amun (of Luxor) temple (Alexander 1999: 57; Plumley 1964: 3-4). This appears to be the only evidence remotely suggesting a Amun temple on site, especially since the possibility of Amun of *Prm*, mentioned in the temple at Kalabsha (Gauthier 1911: 112-113), being worshipped at Qasr Ibrim was made invalid when Caminos (1968: 4) and Meeks (1972: 121) refuted the earlier association made by Brugsch in his *Dictionnaire géographique* (1879: 1161, 1242) between *Prm/Prmt* and Primis, the Greek name of Ibrim.

Additionally, despite some New Kingdom material found at Qasr Ibrim—notably the blocks mentioned above and Ramesside statuary discovered in the temple formerly known as House 1030—there is no firm evidence of occupation prior to the Twenty-fifth Dynasty (Driskell *et al.* 1989:19).

Although the ruins of several temples dated to Napatan and Meroitic periods have been discovered and excavated

---

[11] According to Dewachter (1987: 190), the temple's dedication to Re-Horakhty and Amun-Re is still a common belief among Egyptologists today. The present author revised her original position on this topic and now follows Dewachter's hypothesis.
[12] This chamber is labelled J in Barget *et al.* 1967, pl. 1 but C in Gauthier 1913-26, pl. A and PM VII: 66.

at Qasr Ibrim since 1964 (Alexander and Driskell 1985: 23-26; Alexander 1999: 55-59; R.D. Anderson *et al.* 1979: 31-33; Driskell *et al.* 1989: 11-34), none has thus far been associated with Amun. We note a small multi-room temple built by Taharqo (later transformed into a church) and a much larger Meroitic temple that stood perpendicular to it. The foundation deposits of the Taharqo temple revealed cartouches of this king (Alexander and Driskell 1985: 25) but not the identity of the deity worshipped within its walls. The painted mud plaster fragments recovered from the Meroitic temple (Alexander and Driskell 1985: 26) did not depict the god housed within.

Gebel Adda
The temple erected in the northern section of the acropolis at Gebel Adda, the plan of which appears in Millet's Ph.D. thesis (1968), was thought to be a sacred building dedicated to Amun (Millet 1984: 119). A few small artefacts suggested that it might have been consecrated to the worship of Amun, one of them being a carved wooden sceptre-head in the shape of a shrine decorated with figures of Amun of Napata, Mut, and Horus. The other finds included an extremely weather-worn sandstone head of Sebiumeker (previously identified as a Meroitic ruler wearing a double crown), a shattered sandstone altar, papyri, parchment fragments in cursive Meroitic, and one illustration of a crowned royal figure with empty cartouches. Additionally, two large stelae set within the temple area were uncovered. Unfortunately, both were extremely weather-worn and indecipherable. Only a few signs allowed the slabs of stone to be identified as official stelae. In addition to these few artefacts, several graffiti of Amani were found and reported by Millet in 1984 at the nearby site of Gebel esh-Shems, south of Gebel Adda. Evidence seems to indicate the worship of this god in the area; however, it is not directly related to the building itself and therefore too circumstantial to support the dedication of this temple to the god Amun.

Sesebi
Constructed prior to his Regnal Year 6, Amenhotep IV's triple temple at Sesebi, of which only three columns are still standing, is an intriguing construction. The building consisted of three contiguous temples with a platform pronaos (Blackman 1937: 146-147), the central temple being slightly larger than the two adjoining ones on either side. Seti I later transformed the central sanctuary into a pronaos and had a small sanctuary built behind it (Badawy 1968: 274). Although this temple is often said to be dedicated to the Theban Triad, this is extrapolated from an inscribed door jamb of the northern temple that bore the name of the goddess Mut (Badawy 1968: 275; Blackman 1937: 147; Mostafa 1992: 147; PM VII: 172) and two very small (5 cm), unfinished steatite sculptures of rams found in the central temple (Blackman 1937: 147). Dug below the central temple was a mysterious crypt, the walls of which were decorated with Amenhotep IV in company of Geb, Shu, Osiris, Atum, and Maat-Rē (perhaps Neb-Maat-Rē?) (Blackman 1937: 149). Certain scholars, including the author, are somewhat hesitant to declare this construction a temple dedicated to the Theban Triad because of its very unusual features and the lack of epigraphic materials confirming this, although others see no objections to this idea (Guermeur 2005: 500).

Soniyat
Although the temple at Soniyat, located in the *mantiqa* of Tergis, has never been called an Amun temple *per se*, its internal spatial configuration is strikingly similar to that of the core of the Great Temple of Amun at Gebel Barkal (B500), dated to the reign of Kings Tutankhamun or Horemheb (Żurawski 1998: 183), as well as other New Kingdom temples in Nubia (Żurawski 2003: 245). This peculiarity justified its inclusion in the overall corpus, but cannot fully support a certifiable dedication.

Hugeir Gubli
Very little actually remains of the temple located in the courtyard of Ali Abd Er-Rahim at Hugeir Gubli. However, the size of the foundation blocks and the column bases suggest that the temple was of considerable size. Despite the few traces of polychrome decoration on the blocks used to build a modern dyke to fence off Ali Abd Er-Rahim's house from the river, the ruins themselves have not revealed much (Żurawski 2003: 358-360). However, the excavators think the Hugeir temple is to be equated with the temple complex of Amun of Tara-on-ensi mentioned in the Annals of Harsiotef, dated to his Regnal Year 35 (Żurawski 2001: 286; FHN II: 443). Across the Nile exactly opposite Hugeir, a smaller but better-preserved temple was discovered at Usli, along with Napatan ceramics and imported Egyptian marl wares (Żurawski 2001: 285). This small temple is thought to be the Temple of Bastet of Tare because a bronze feline figurine (either Bastet or Sekhmet) had been found in the Usli graveyard. The small temple of Bastet of Tare is also mentioned in the Annals of Harsiotef and the Nastasen Stela. This temple was the one from which Harsiotef went down to the temple of Amun of Tara-on-ensi (Żurawski 2001: 286). Although these associations are very compelling, neither temple has been positively identified yet.

Mutmir
Hintze described the site of Mutmir as a large mound covered with fragments of red bricks, flat black sandstone (ferricrete) slabs as well as remains of column drums and pillars. Some fragments of sandstone were carved with recognisable reliefs. The pottery assemblage was composed of Classic and Late Meroitic sherds. Based on the surface remains, Hintze has suggested that there might be a Meroitic temple on site (1959: 174). This site was tentatively identified by Priese as Sakarage (*s-k3-r-g3-t*), mentioned in the Harsiotef inscription, a site that played an important role in the Procession Festival of

Amun and Osiris (1984c: 496). Until the site of Mutmir is confirmed as being the ancient Sakarage and, more importantly, the temple located and Amun identified as the deity honoured within, this Meroitic site cannot be listed as including an Amun temple.

Meroe KC104
The small temple located south of the processional avenue leading towards the Amun Temple M260 at Meroe is an unusual construction: a double temple with a suite of central rooms of unknown function. Zach and Tomandl have mentioned that it could potentially be a structure dedicated to Amun; however, the authors have also indicated that the building might also be associated with Isis, Hathor, and Mut (2000: 136). Shinnie and Anderson abstained from associating the structure with a specific deity as archaeological evidence does not support any such claim.

Meroe M250 (Sun Temple)
The so-called Sun Temple at Meroe bears a misleading name because as far as we know, sun worship did not exist in Meroitic religion (Hakem 1988: 191; Hinkel 2001: 6). Sayce associated Herodotus' "Table of the Sun" with "Temple of the Sun," and thought that M250 was this building (Hakem 1988: 191; Hinkel 2001: 6). The architectural plan of this small peripteral temple denoted Graeco-Roman influences, but greatly resembled single-room Meroitic temples. Preserved reliefs show battle scenes of captives slain by the king, the king triumphantly returning in his chariot, and processions of horsemen and soldiers (Hakem 1988: 204-207; PM VII: 239, Török 1997a: 103). Standing in front of Prince Akinidad, one of the figures was tentatively identified with Amun; the deity wore a red crown with twisted horizontal horns mounted with a uraeus (Török 1997a: 105). However, certain scholars believe that a deified Meroitic ruler or ancestor could instead be venerated in this temple (Zach 1999: 690-693).

Hinkel suggested that the temple was dedicated to Amun simply because its measurements were multiples of the Egyptian cubit, not the Greek module (Hinkel 2001: 7). While it might be postulated that the temple was dedicated to an Egyptian deity based on the measuring unit, the identity of that deity cannot be determined. As the temple dedicated to Isis (M600) demonstrates, Amun was not the only Egyptian deity worshipped at Meroe. Moreover, it should not be forgotten that "old" measuring units can still be used even when "new" ones have officially been introduced, making the situation even more confusing. Ultimately, the author believes that the current evidence is too circumstantial to support the claim that M250 is an Amun Temple.

Meroe Early Amun Temple (Royal City M292-298)
Within the Royal City Enclosure, Garstang discovered the remnants of a small chapel (M292), while fragments of columns and roof slabs presumably originating from a temple were unearthed in the vicinity (buildings 293-298) (Garstang 1912; Török 1997a: 145ff). Archaeological evidence—inscribed sandstone fragments and votive objects with cartouches of early Napatan kings—indicated the presence of an early Napatan building on site. Török suggested that an early Amun temple existed at Meroe prior to the construction of the Great Amun Temple M260, and that it was in fact located in the Royal City in areas M292-M298 (Török 1997a: 29, 146). However, the archaeological evidence to support the claim that M292 formed part of the early Amun temple remains inconclusive.

Meroe M600 (Isis Temple)
Three construction phases were identified on the site of the small temple M600. Although this temple was dedicated to Isis during the Meroitic period (based on a votive stela of Teriteqas adoring Isis as well as statues of the goddess found inside), Zach and Tomandl, based on Török's interpretation, believe this building was originally dedicated to Amun during early Napatan times (Zach and Tomandl 2000: 134). According to Török, the structure of the early construction phase of M600 bore similarities to the spatial configuration of the core of the large Amun Temple M260, the orientation was the same, and even the measurements were almost identical (1984a: 351-356). Hakem suggested that the structure next to the main building was in fact a temple to Apedemak (1988: 36). The main temple was also fronted by two colossal statues of Sebiumeker and Arensnuphis (Török 1997a: 170ff). Garstang's plan is confusing at best and evidence is inconclusive at the moment.

Meroe M720
Temple M720, another of the M260 avenue temples, was discovered by Garstang and only partially excavated; however, it was not until Shinnie's excavation on site in the mid-1970s that this temple was fully documented. Two sandstone blocks carved with a partial representation of Amanitore before the ram-headed god were found within the temple (Török 1997a: 178). Based on these decorated fragments and the temple's spatial organisation, some scholars have tentatively identified the structure as a small Amun temple (Wenig 1984: 389; Zach and Tomandl 2000: 134). Zach and Tomandl have also suggested a dedication to Thoth because a statue of this deity was found in the temple (2000: 134). However, Shinnie and Anderson's recent publication confirmed that no artefactual or epigraphic evidence suggests the identification of the deities to which the temples along the processional avenue were dedicated (2004: 65).

Hamadab H1000
The religious structure H1000 (formerly M1000) at Hamadab was identified by Sayce, who worked with Garstang in 1914, as a shrine dedicated to Hapi of Bigga and Osiris (Garstang 1916: 15). Although he did not elaborate on the reasons for his choice of deity, it has been shown that his reasoning was based on his

interpretation of the two great stelae of Hamadab, the Akinidad and Amanirenas stelae, which Garstang had discovered that season. Lloyd, in a short communication in 1970, demonstrated that indeed Sayce's attribution was based on literary not archaeological evidence and that his interpretation of the Meroitic stelae was wrong. Griffith, as Lloyd points out, also attempted to decipher the stelae and his rendering of the text was quite different from that of Sayce. Griffith never came across the name "Hapi of Bigga" or "Osiris."

More recently, Zach and Tomandl (2000: 132) have attributed the small shrine to Amun, claiming that the inscriptions on the stelae were unequivocally addressed to that god. The names *Amn* and *Amnp* are indeed recognisable in the Akinidad Stela text, and they appear together with the words *qor* (ruler) and *mlo* (good)/*lḫ* (big, great) (FHN II: 719-723). Additional support for this claim is the fact that stelae were generally erected in front of monumental temples dedicated to Amun (Zach and Tomandl 2000: 132). The presence of these two stelae needs explanation, especially because the presence of a large temple has yet to be discovered (Wolf 2006: 252). Wolf has suggested that a large building might still be uncovered under the South Mound (Wolf 2003: 106). As tempting as it may be to attribute this small building to Amun, the rest of the inscription has not been deciphered and the context in which the name of the god appears cannot be determined, and cannot be used with any certainty to dedicate the building to him. Even Wolf, the director of the German excavations at Hamadab, hesitates in officially identifying this construction as an Amun shrine. The function of this structure has yet to be determined, but it has been suggested by Wolf in his latest site reports (2002a and 2002b) and in a subsequent conference paper (2006) that it might be military in nature, celebrating a different side of Amun—his warrior aspect. Indeed, the architectural remains of the northern *kôm* where H1000 was located showed interesting similarities to Roman *castra* (fortified military camps) in Egypt (2002b; 2006: 252). Roman castra had a standardised rectangular plan with a large monumental gate and a shrine situated opposite this main gate, at the other end of the *via praetoria* (Curl 1999: 133; Wolf 2006: 252). Small finds, like archers' looses, support this understanding of the building's function primarily as military. Additionally, what is currently understood or extrapolated from the Akinidad Stela concerns the military conflict between Meroe and Rome, which strengthens the hypothesis even more (Wolf 2006: 252).

Yet, certain scholars have associated this building with the god Apedemak, rather than with Amun. Garstang discovered two small sandstone lion statues (1916: 15), which stood "guarding the inner entrance" of the shrine (Hakem 1988: 45). In fact, Hakem classified this temple as a "lion temple" (1988: 47).

Awlib
The site of Awlib, which is much larger than previously thought, consists of several large mounds, the largest of which revealed a small temple (*Kôm* A) (Borcowski 2003: 82-83). Numerous sandstone fragments, including a relief fragment depicting the double-feathered crown of Amun, a winged sun disk, *ḫkr*-frieze, and water lines, as well as great quantities of red bricks and plaster were found on site. Inscriptions in Egyptian hieroglyphs date the structure to the Napatan period. The surface finds support the idea of a Napatan temple on site, one possibly dedicated to Amun, as indicated by Zach and Tomandl (2000: 136). The state of the current excavation shows that this small temple was a tripartite temple of Egyptian influence. Smaller mounds parallel to the axis of the main mound bear a resemblance to the processional avenue leading up to the Temple of Amun (M260) at Meroe. Nonetheless, there is no evidence at present that supports a dedication to Amun; the hieroglyphic material is not diagnostic enough to warrant such a claim (Paner: personal communication).

Wad ban Naga WBN300
Lepsius' Prussian Expedition at Wad ban Naga noticed similarities between the remains of the temple on *Kôm* C and those of the Amun Temple at Naga, which they had just surveyed (Priese 1984a: 18-20; 1984b: 347). However, due to the discovery of three barque stands, one of which was inscribed with the name "Isis, Lady of the Underworld" (REM 0041), it was thought that the building was dedicated to her. Yet, the position of the barque stand—in the north chamber of the second vestibule as opposed to the main sanctuary—would indicate that Isis was not the main cult deity, but a guest in the temple (Priese 1984a: 19; 1984b: 347). The same applied to Hathor, whose name was inscribed on one of the other barque stands (Priese 1984a: 19, 25ff; 1984b: 347; Zach and Tomandl 2000: 131). Therefore, the so-called Isis Temple of Wad ban Naga would not be dedicated solely to this great goddess. Zach and Tomandl have proposed that both Hathor and Isis had guest cults in a temple dedicated to Amun, where his Osirian aspect was worshipped (2000: 131). Other than the similarity in plan between WBN300 and N100, there is no evidence linking Amun to this particular structure at Wad ban Naga.[13]

Wad ban Naga WBN500
Temple WBN500, also known as the Eastern Temple, at Wad ban Naga is labelled "Amun Temple" on Hakem's map (1988: 317). However, he does not give any reason why the temple is so marked and neither does Hinkel (1997: 398), except that multi-room temples are generally thought to be dedicated solely to Egyptian deities. Vercoutter abstained from making suggestions about the dedication in his site reports (1962b).

---

[13] The architectural plan of the Amun Temple at Naga has changed—albeit not drastically—since the publication of Priese's article. Most of the similarities are still noticeable.

Alem

According to Zach and Tomandl (2000: 136), a two-chamber temple at a small Meroitic site 16 km north of Meroe was dedicated to Amun. However, no evidence was given to support this claim. Hinkel, amongst other scholars, visited and studied the site, and did not mention any evidence of this dedication. The structure is completely destroyed and the adhering plaster on some of the fragments and features did not reveal a decorative program that could be reconstructed.

Duanib

The now-destroyed single-room Meroitic temple, which was described by Cailliaud during his *Voyage à Méroé* (1826, vol. III: 158) and Lepsius in his *Denkmäler* (I: 140), was attributed to Amun by Zach and Tomandl, based on the depictions on the blocks (Zach and Tomandl 2000: 143). One of the reliefs described by Lepsius shows a male deity on a throne accompanied by a goddess standing behind and the royal family standing in front. Although the heads are missing, Zach and Tomandl have suggested that this male deity is Amun based on the features of the throne upon which he sits. This type of throne is dated to the reign of Natakamani and Amanitore.

A second temple, also destroyed, was noted by Lepsius and later by Hintze. Wenig indicated that the temple appears to be a multi-roomed temple and this, according to his typology, indicates that it was dedicated to an Egyptian deity (Wenig: personal communication). The name of Amun is not mentioned in relation to this temple.

Musawwarat es-Sufra IA-100

The Great Enclosure at Musawwarat es-Sufra is one of the most enigmatic structures of all of Meroitic Sudan. The clusters of individual buildings were linked together with corridors and terraces, and the centre of this architectural complex was labelled Temple IA 100. Although the function of the Great Enclosure has yet to be elucidated, the central unit is now believed by most archaeologists to be a small temple or shrine. Hintze suggested that this small temple was dedicated to Amun; his hypothesis was supported by the two triple-protomes found at the entrance of the temple (1968: 676). The famous triple-protomes of Musawwarat were part of the architectural sculptural tradition of the site. The protome associated with the main entrance of IA 100 represented the head of an *ovis platyra aegyptiaca* ram (probably Amun) wearing a sun disc and two uraei, flanked by the human heads of the guardian gods Arensnuphis and Sebiumeker (Wenig 2001: 80). The second protome was installed above the side entrance, but was found in several fragments that were reconstructed as an *ovis platyra aegyptiaca* ram flanked this time by two goddesses, perhaps Isis and Hathor or Nephthys (Wenig 2001: 80). However, there is no epigraphic material inside the temple that even slightly suggests that it was dedicated to Amun in any of his forms.

Amun of Nowhere

An inscription in the temple of Kalabsha makes reference to Amun of *Prm* (Gauthier 1911: 112-113), which, in his *Dictionnaire géographique* (1879: 1161, 1242), Brugsch associated with Primis, the Greek name of Qasr Ibrim. *Prm* was never equated with Ibrim in any inscription coming from that site, and this earlier association was refuted by Caminos (1968: 4) and Meeks (1972: 121). Furthermore, the archaeological evidence does not support the existence of Amun temple at Ibrim (see Qasr Ibrim above).

Amun of Takhompso is mentioned on a red granite barque stand (altar) found at in the Temple of Isis at Philae (Weigall 1907: 49; Griffith 1930:128-129). The precise location of Takhompso has never been identified with certainty. Certain scholars (notably Griffith 1930: 129 and Sethe 1964: 3) have equated Takhompso with Philae, based on the find location of the Taharqo barque stand and the fact that Herodotus (Book II, ch. 29; for commentary, see Lloyd 1976: 118-120) appears to have confused Takhompso with Philae. The most logical site, according to Lloyd, is the Island of Djerar (1976:118-120). Neither *Prm* nor Takhompso have been archaeologically discovered and officially identified. For this reason, they are simply worth a mention in this chapter.

SUMMARY

Table 1 summarises the results of this study. In all of Nubia, the current archaeological record shows that 31 known sites have been associated with the cult of the god Amun in one way or another. At these sites, the presence of 43 temples has been postulated; however, only 38 have actually been discovered. Among these 38 temples, only 18 were positively identified as Amun temples (18/38). Seven of these temples were built during the Egyptian New Kingdom (7/18), five during the Twenty-fifth Dynasty/Napatan period (5/18) and eight were the results of Meroitic endeavours (8/18).

Of the seven New Kingdom temples, two of them were enlarged (Gebel Barkal B500) or annexed to a new construction (Doukki Gel West Temple and Annexes/West and East Temples, Napatan phase) during the Napata period. These two structures were also refurbished during the Meroitic period, together with Napatan buildings at Gebel Barkal, B700 and B800. This emphasises the importance of both Gebel Barkal and Kerma/Doukki Gel in the religious life of both the Egyptians and the Kushites.

Table 1: Identification of Amun Temples

Site Name	Temple	Period	Positive Cult ID Rams	Positive Cult ID Inscriptions	Inconclusive ID
Dabod	Chapel of Amun	MR		✓	
Amada	Temple of Rē-Horakhty	NK			x
Aniba	No Amun temple discovered	NK			x
Qasr Ibrim	No NK temple discovered	NK			x
Gebel Adda	Meroitic Temple	MR			x
Aksha	Temple of Amun, Rē and Ramses II	NK		✓	
Amara East	Temple of Amun	MR		✓	
Amara West	Temple of Amun-Rē	NK		✓	
Sai Island	Temple A	NK		✓	
Soleb	Temple of Amun and Nebmaatrē	NK	✓	✓	
Sesebi	Triple Temple of Theban Triad	NK			x
Tabo	Postulated Temple of Amun of Pnubs	Dyn. 25			x
Doukki Gel	Temple Complex of Amun of Pnubs				
	>West Temple	NK		✓	
	>West Temple and Annexes	Dyn. 25		✓	
	>West and East Temples	NP/MR		✓	
Kawa	Temple A	NK		✓	
	Temple B	MR		✓	
	Temple T	Dyn.25	✓	✓	
Soniyat	Temple TRG40	NP/MR			x
Hugeir Gubli	Temple of Amun Tara-on-ensi?	NP			x
Gebel Barkal	B500	NK/Dyn. 25 / NP/MR	✓	✓	
	B700	NP/MR		✓	
	B800 (First/Second)	NP/MR	✓		
Sanam	Temple of Amun, Bull of Nubia	Dyn. 25		✓	
Dangeil	Temple of Amun	MR	✓		
Mutmir	No temple discovered	MR			x
Meroe	KC104	MR			x
	M250	MR			x
	M260	MR	✓	✓	
	M292-298	NP/MR			x
	M600	NP/MR			x
	M720	MR			x
Hamadab	H1000	MR			x
Awlib	Postulated Temple of Amun	NP/MR?			x
el-Hassa	Temple of Amun of Tabakh	MR	✓		
Wad ban Naga	WBN300	MR			x
	WBN500	MR			x
Alem	Meroitic Temple	MR			x
Duanib	Temple I	MR			x
Musawwarat	Temple IA 100	MR			x
Naga	N100	MR	✓	✓	
	N500	MR		✓	
Umm Soda	No temple discovered	MR	✓		
Soba	No temple discovered	NP/MR	✓		

Legend: NK = New Kingdom, Dyn 25 = Twenty-fifth Dynasty, NP = Napatan, and MR = Meroitic.

CHAPTER 4. TYPOLOGY OF AMUN TEMPLES IN NUBIA

INTRODUCTION

Typology, the classification of entities into categories based on similar characteristics, is a well-known approach in the field of archaeology. In fact, "not only is it fundamental to all scientific disciplines, it lies at the core of human conceptualization of the real world by identifying, organizing, and naming different kinds of things" (Rice 1987: 274). As with artefacts, a typological study of architectural structures is a valid method for the study of architectural development and the evaluation of possible influences from one historical period to the next. With regard to the conclusively identified Amun temples in the corpus, it is the formal aspect of the architectural structures that is the focus of the study—in other words, the architectural plan, the spatial configuration, the layout of the various rooms and courts.

Once the study corpus has been established, the creation of a formal classification scheme is the next step in the typological research process. As mentioned by Rice, it is impossible for a classification system to account for and accommodate all the characteristics of the entities under study, even though some scholars claim that a classification should do so in order to be considered valid (1987: 276). A method of sorting currently in favour in Nubian studies is the sorting in stages, where an initial division into a few broad classes is followed by a further subdivision of refined categories and a final division into types (Adams and Adams 1991: 199). Intuition, deductive reasoning, and a basic knowledge of temple architecture allow the identification of the fundamental characteristics of an Egyptian, Napatan, or Meroitic temple, as well as the particular features that are common to a fraction of the corpus. The result of the main typological exercise is described and explained in greater detail below (see Table 2).

TYPOLOGY OF AMUN TEMPLES:[14]
DESCRIPTION OF THE CLASSIFICATION SCHEME

Within the temple assemblage, an immediate split into two fundamental groups occurs at the onset of the study. This most crucial division resides in the fundamental spatial configuration of the temple plan: an edifice comprising at its most basic level several rooms linked together or a building consisting of one single room. Most New Kingdom and Napatan temples were based on the former, the axial tripartite plan, where three sections are identified: the columnar courts, the vestibule (occasionally a columned pronaos), and the sanctuary area. While the multi-room temple still remained in favour, the single-room temple became popular during Meroitic times. This temple was, however, generally associated with local deities rather than with Egyptian gods and goddesses. Although the majority of these Meroitic single-room temples were indeed dedicated to the Nubian lion god Apedemak, Amun was also worshipped in these small temples, even though there are much fewer buildings of that size dedicated to him.

DIVISION 1, GROUP A: SINGLE-ROOM TEMPLES

As the name implies, the single-room temple comprises only one chamber. The altar, upon which the naos containing the statue of the deity rests or where libations and offerings were performed, was often located in that one room. Occasionally, a small niche where the deity's statue stood was carved in the back wall, facing towards the massive pylon entrance, and a portico was erected in front of the temple. These particular features, although notable, are not "significant" variants in the elaboration of the type itself.

Group A, Regular Type
Members of this group: Dabod and Naga N500

Only one type can be determined for this group: the regular single-room temple. This type comprises only two buildings, the chapel of Amun at Dabod and Naga 500. Both these temples belong in the single-room temple group without any further subdivision.

The chapel of Amun at Dabod was incorporated into a later Ptolemaic temple erected by Ptolemy VI, which was also dedicated to Amun of *t3-ḥwt* (Dabod) as well as to Isis of the Abaton (Arnold 1999: 179; 2003: 64). Because the small temple was enlarged and incorporated into a larger one, it is difficult to ascertain its original plan. All that is known, however, is that the structure was a single-room building during the time of Adikhalamani.

As for Naga N500, Amun was not the only deity worshipped in this temple. He shared the cult space with another form of himself (?), Apedemak (?) or a divine ruler (?) (Zach and Tomandl 2000: 141; Wolf 2006: 257). The identity of Amun's co-resident has yet to be determined, but Amun did dwell in a one-room building at the foot of Gebel Naga. A columned portico fronted the entrance pylon. A niche for the cult statue was carved in the far wall, immediately opposite the entrance.

DIVISION 1, GROUP B: MULTI-ROOM TEMPLES

In the study of Meroitic architecture, the term "Amun temple" is often used to refer to large multi-room temples, but this usage—notably by Hakem—is somewhat misleading because not all of the multi-room temples were dedicated to Amun. Wenig and Adams pointed out that, instead, the term "multi-room" should be

---

[14] The typology is slightly different from an earlier version presented at the *Conférence internationale d'études méroïtiques* held in Paris in 2004.

used as a descriptive term for Egyptianising temples, as opposed to Meroitic single-room temples (Adams 1984: 258; Wenig 1984: 384). Still, the term should be solely used as an adjective from a spatial configuration point of view without any connotation to specific deities or specific historical periods because otherwise, as pointed out by Wolf (2006: 240), it is too discriminating.

In contrast to single-room or two-room temples—none of the latter has been officially accepted as Amun temples in the previous chapter—the multi-room temples were composed of three or more rooms. In this respect, they virtually always follow the linear Egyptian tripartite plan. A number of spatial configuration possibilities occurred with the multi-room temples and, as Wenig (1984) concluded in his own typology, this group could be further divided. The present corpus could be subdivided in two groups.

DIVISION 2, GROUP B.1:
MULTI-ROOM WITH BASIC PLAN

The simplest possible version of the multi-room temple—the basic multi-room—comprises a court (the open/semi-public space), a vestibule (the buffer zone), and the sanctuary area (the sacred space). Such temples were generally conceived on this plan from the start and were usually smaller than Group B.2 temples. The basic multi-room group roughly corresponds to Wenig's Type B and can be equated with Wolf's "small multi-room temple." There was only one type of temple in the basic multi-room group, the regular type.

Several configurations of sanctuaries were noticed among the temples in the corpus, notably within this type—single sanctuary, perambulatory sanctuary, niched sanctuary, double or triple sanctuary. It is most important to note that different sanctuary configurations within this or any other type are simply a variant of the type. All temples, even grouped in sub-types, are actually all secure members of the actual type. These variations of the sanctuary configuration were judged noteworthy because they occur in each type (see Chapter 5, the Single Sanctuary versus Triple Sanctuary discussion), with the exception of the jubilee type where there is only one member. Concurrently, such variants help in determining architectural models and they therefore must be noted. The sub-type variants do not undermine the type in any way.

Group B.1: Regular Type
Members of this type: B700, Kawa Temple B, Aksha, B500 (core), and Sai Temple A.

B.1 Regular Type/Sub-type (i): Niched Sanctuary
The temples classified in this category show that there was a niche in a wall or that a very small room that protruded at the back of the edifice. This small chamber was so reduced in space that it barely contains an altar. The small temple B700 at Gebel Barkal is the best example.

B.1, Regular Type/Sub-type (ii): Single Sanctuary
The single sanctuary, unlike the niched sanctuary, does not protrude at the back of the temple; it consists of a single room that uses the back wall of the temple as its own wall. In a number of temples, the single sanctuary could actually be surrounded by additional subsidiary chambers (not to be confused with the side sanctuaries of the triple sanctuary sub-type) or it can be a perambulatory sanctuary in which the sanctuary's back wall is not shared. The example is Temple B at Kawa.

B.1, Regular Type/Sub-type (iii): Triple Sanctuary
The triple sanctuary was a well-attested feature in Amun temples in Nubia: three sanctuaries located side by side far inside the temple, often with the central one being larger than the other two. Significant differences existed in the spatial configuration of the three sanctuaries and the diversity led to the division into three sub-types. Again, it must be noted that variants within the triple sanctuary sub-type do not undermine the type or the sub-type.

Triple Sanctuary Configuration (a): Plain
The plain triple sanctuary is the simplest form of this feature. In this case, as with the temple at Aksha, the three sanctuaries were the same length and reached the far wall. The width often varied between the side sanctuaries and the central one, but the important characteristic was the plainness of the small rooms, where no division and *enfilade* of rooms occurred.

Triple Sanctuary Configuration (b): Divided
The divided triple sanctuary can be recognised by its division into smaller rooms, where door jambs are clearly visible between each little chamber. The divisions are varied and numerous, but the important feature is that the sanctuaries are divided into smaller chambers and are interconnected with one another in some way. The core of the Great Temple of Amun at Gebel Barkal (B500), built during the reign of Tutankhamun or Horemheb, displayed this particular type of sanctuary.

Triple Sanctuary Configuration (c): Complex
The maze-like sanctuary at Sai Island's Temple A illustrates well the complex triple sanctuary configuration. Not only is the south side sanctuary divided, it leads into a small transverse chamber located behind the central sanctuary, thus making it shorter than the north side sanctuary. Once again, variation in the division of the sanctuaries into smaller units may occur.

DIVISION 2, GROUP B.2:
MULTI-ROOM WITH COMPLEX PLAN

The complex multi-room plan is self-explanatory: the architectural plan of the temple is more elaborate than the basic plan mentioned above. The major difference resides in the number of courts and, occasionally, in the additional subsidiary chambers around these courts and the sanctuary area. This group corresponds to Wenig's Type A and can be equated to Wolf's "large multi-room temples." Several of these complex multi-room temples were constructed with a particular layout in mind; in other words, their complexity was not the result of growth by accretion. Other sacred buildings were, however, modified extensively during the centuries and their final architectural plan was the result of a number of kings' contributions to the cult of their father, Amun. The best example of the latter process in Nubia is the Great Temple of Amun of Napata at Gebel Barkal because the various construction phases that occurred at different periods allowed its placement in different types.

The next level of classification must take into account the increased number of rooms before focussing on the sanctuary configuration. The types are described and explained below, and whenever the case, the variant subdivisions are also summarised. Again, this subdivision does not affect the number of secure members within each type.

Group B.2: Regular Type
Members of this type: B800-Second, Kawa A, Amara West, Doukki Gel West Temple (all periods), B800-First, B500 (Ramesside)

The regular complex multi-room is in fact the complex equivalent of the basic multi-room temple, except that in this instance there are more courts along the central axis. On par with its basic counterpart, the regular complex multi-room temple is also divided according to the sanctuary arrangements, variants also found in this type.

B.2, Regular Type/Sub-type (i): Niched Sanctuary
The only temple in this larger version of the basic regular niched sanctuary type is the second phase building of Gebel Barkal B800. Although the niched sanctuary is larger than in B700, for example, the concept is the same. The niche protrudes from the back wall.

B.2, Regular Type/Sub-type (ii): Single Sanctuary
Temple Kawa A is the only example in this category. The plan is difficult to make out because the links between the rooms in the sanctuary area are not well defined. The single sanctuary is intriguing; the vestibule is practically part of the sanctuary itself. Additionally, the earlier stone structure built by Tutankhamun was very badly incorporated into an edifice erected by Taharqo. Nonetheless, despite its odd architectural planning, Kawa A fits in this category.

B.2, Regular Type/Sub-type (iii): Triple Sanctuary
Once again, this is a larger version of the same type in Group B.1. The sanctuary configurations follow the same patterns described above:

Sub-type (iii) Triple Sanctuary—Configuration (a): Plain
As mentioned previously, the similarity between the regular complex multi-room and the basic multi-room temple is striking. Most of the time, it is the addition of one or more courts to the *enfilade* that classifies a temple in this category. The case of Amara West speaks for itself: the temple had three plain sanctuaries, a vestibule, a hypostyle hall, an additional peristyle court as well as a large open court without a pylon. The first building phase of Gebel Barkal B800 was also constructed along these lines, even if it is off-axis.

Sub-type (iii) Triple Sanctuary—Configuration (b): Divided
The numerous construction phases of the Great Temple of Amun at Gebel Barkal (B500) make it an excellent example to illustrate various types of temples. The core of the temple was mentioned above as an example of the basic multi-room with divided triple sanctuary. A later New Kingdom addition by Ramses II—the columnar hall numbered 503 on Reisner and Dunham's plans—turned the small temple into a complex multi-room temple with a divided triple sanctuary, which is the category described here. The West Temple at Doukki Gel—the only temple from this site that could be sorted—also fits in this category.

Group B.2: Jubilee Type
Members of this type: Soleb

Amongst all the Amun temples of Nubia, the jubilee temple of Amenhotep III is an architectural masterpiece without equal. Despite the fact that it generally follows the complex multi-room with divided triple sanctuary, the presence of the sun court, the numerous columns erected in the various sanctuaries, and the presence of a perambulatory shrine in the central unit give it a type of its own

Additionally, the facts that it functioned as a jubilee temple in honour of Amenhotep III and his various exploits, and that the king's own deified person was worshipped within the building during his lifetime (Kozloff and Bryan 1992: 106-108), give this Amun temple its own special status.

Group B.2: Coronation Type
Members of this type: B500 (Piankhy), Kawa T, Sanam, and M260

Taharqo's coronation temples undoubtedly are the Kushite temples subjected to the most intense scholarly research. The temples at Kawa (Kawa T) and Sanam follow an identical architectural plan, where two courts (the first peristyle and the second hypostyle) precede a pronaos and a single sanctuary in a linear fashion along the temple's axis. The coronation temple's distinguishing characteristic was the dais room (also called a "throne room") found on the south side of the sanctuary and the distinctive configuration of the auxiliary chambers on the other side. These two temples were conceived with this complex architectural structure in mind and erected as a single and complete unit.

The Amun Temple at Gebel Barkal (B500) became, from the reign of Piankhy onwards, a coronation temple, although it obtained this status only through extensive modifications. King Piankhy not only added two additional forecourts, he also erected a dais room south of the columned court of Tutankhamun. Considering that the temple was not originally built as a coronation temple at the onset of construction, its plan is not as integrated as are those of Taharqo.

As for the temple of Amun of Pnubs, it will be discussed in greater detail in the next chapter (Chapter 5 – Some Remaining Issues) because the ruinous conditions of the East Temple does not allow for proper categorisation. At the same time, its amalgamation with the West Temple is subject to interpretation.

The Amun Temple at Meroe (M260) was never associated with the coronation journey and its related celebrations on any of the royal stelae. However, its importance as the residence of the royal brethren is made clear on the stelae of Irike-Amanote (FNH II: 401) and Nastasen (FHN II: 475). According to Hakem, this would denote the importance of Meroe as the capital of the kingdom and indicate a departure point for the coronation journey (1988: 150).

Nonetheless, because of its architectural configuration, Temple M260 has always been considered by scholars as a coronation temple. The structure of the building's core appeared to be, after a brief visual inspection, a mixture of Piankhy's B500 and Taharqo's Kawa T temples. An analogy with B500 is possible; the dais room is located on the south side of the sanctuary. The layout of the room itself is strikingly similar: a dais with a few steps, fronted with two rows of four columns, all of which are located in a rectangular room. In contrast, the dais rooms at Kawa and Sanam differed slightly; the room itself is not rectangular and the configuration is divergent. The dais is located in a small and restrictive space on the right-hand side of the door, while one row of four columns occupies the wider and longer space on the left. However, just like Taharqo's temples, M260 has a small transverse room behind the sanctuary. Indeed, M260 resembles Kawa T and Sanam more than B500, simply because it appears to have been constructed as a unit (and has undergone very little renovations or changes) instead of having grown into a coronation temple by accretion.

Group B.2: Amanitore Type
Members of this type: Naga 100, Dangeil, and Amara East

The Amanitore type temple is named after the great queen whose name is found on artefacts discovered at the temple site or on the actual structures that follow this particular architectural plan. Certain scholars might prefer to call it the "Natakamani Type," which, all in all, would be exactly the same. Queen Amanitore and King Natakamani, the most architecturally prolific royal couple of the Meroitic period, commissioned architectural projects together and both their names appear on their monuments. Although a name based on the temple's function (like the jubilee or coronation type) would be more appropriate, the specific function of this temple type has yet to be determined.

The architectural layout of the Amanitore temple is, like the coronation temples, very distinctive. It consists of a large pylon gateway that leads into the first court, a transverse hypostyle hall. Two smaller columned courts of identical width, although they are not necessarily of the same length, follow this hall. The second of these smaller courts gives access to very elongated lateral chambers as well as the sanctuary area. The Amanitore temple plan also includes a differently configured dais room (in the north elongated lateral room) and this noteworthy fact shall be discussed in Chapter 5 – Some Remaining Issues.

Three temples were classified as Amanitore type temples, those being at Naga (N100), Dangeil, and Amara East. Although the temple at Amara East was almost entirely destroyed when it was first recorded by early travellers and archaeologists, the plan given by Lepsius (the most elaborate of all plans published) shows two rooms of identical width. This single characteristic, in addition to the facts that the temple was indeed erected by Amanitore and Natakamani, and that it was dedicated to Amun, allows it to be classified here in spite of the incomplete architectural plan. Needless to say, it was impossible to classify the Amara East temple into further sub-categories because the sanctuary area is destroyed. Yet, it can be proposed that it belongs in the Amanitore complex multi-room temple group.

Amanitore Type/Sub-type (i): Single Sanctuary
At Naga, only one sanctuary is accessible from the preceding room, the pronaos. The side chambers located on either side of the main sanctuary are not accessible from this room at all. In fact, they could only be reached from the lateral chambers, which were accessible from the pronaos.

Amanitore Type/Sub-type (iii) Triple Sanctuary – Configuration (a) Plain
In the case of Dangeil, there are three sanctuaries accessible from the pronaos, in the manner described for the basic multi-room temple. The central sanctuary is slightly larger than the side ones. A pink sandstone altar, now smashed to pieces, was located in this central sanctuary.

ADDITIONAL CLASSIFICATION EXERCISE

The architectural plans of a number of buildings inconclusively identified as Amun temples actually fit in the newly established classification scheme. Although the identification of an Amun temple cannot be determined with certainty based solely on its spatial configuration, it certainly strengthens the possibility. As an additional classification exercise to test the typology, the few inconclusively identified temples that share architectural characteristics with those in the typology have been classified within it (entries highlighted in Table 3). No new categories have been created in the typology to accommodate these temples.

No additional temples could be classified in Group A, the single-room temples, without making significant changes to the typology. However, several other temples could be added to Group B, the multi-room temples. These new additions were almost evenly divided among Group B.1 (basic plan) and Group B.2 (complex plan).

The following temples were classified in B.1, the multi-room basic plan sub-group. The small temple at Awlib was added to the regular temple type, sub-type (iii) triple sanctuary. The sanctuary arrangement was tentatively identified as configuration (a) plain. Evidently, considering the nascent state of the excavations, this classification may change in the near future.

The Napatan and Meroitic temples at Soniyat (the second built on and using the vestige of the first) both fit in the regular type. These two temples were also classified in the triple sanctuary sub-type, but in configuration (b) divided. Their resemblance to the core of Barkal B500 was the reason why they were grouped here. The temple at Amada, where Amun is visually omnipresent in the wall decorations but not in name, can also be added to this type, sub-type and sanctuary configuration.

As for the multi-room complex plan (Group B.2), there were two new additions in this group. Although the site of Tabo cannot be equated with the ancient site of Pnubs, its temple nonetheless still shares characteristics with Taharqo's coronation temples at Kawa and Sanam. Such features are the peristyle court, the hypostyle hall, and the columns in the southernmost room of the sanctuary area. The latter are reminiscent of the columns of the dais rooms at Kawa T and Sanam. Therefore, Tabo could be classified in the coronation type, which is the label it had been given since its discovery.

The Amanitore Type was also augmented with a new temple, Wad ban Naga WBN300, the so-called Isis Temple. Lepsius, and later Priese, noted the resemblance between Naga N100 and WBN300. However, the architectural plan of N100 has since then been modified. As seen by the dotted lines on the drawing (see Figure 36), the plan of WBN300 is almost entirely reconstructed by G. Erbkam, the architect who worked with Lepsius. Much of WBN300 is speculation and the plan could have very well changed had it been studied again in later years, like N100. The fact that Amanitore and Natakamani also built this temple strengthens the possibility of it being dedicated to Amun.

SUMMARY

The positively identified Amun temples in the corpus can indeed be classified neatly into general and more specific categories based on their spatial configuration and specific architectural features. Amun temples tend to follow the general linear tripartite plan, but there are certain modifications and additions suggesting that certain plans were preferable for a specific cult activity. Some of these variations can be dated to a particular historical period or a specific reign. A few temples that were not positively identified as Amun temples have also been grouped within the newly created categories as an additional typological exercise. See Tables 2 and 3 for illustrations of the typology.

Table 2: Typology of Amun Temples

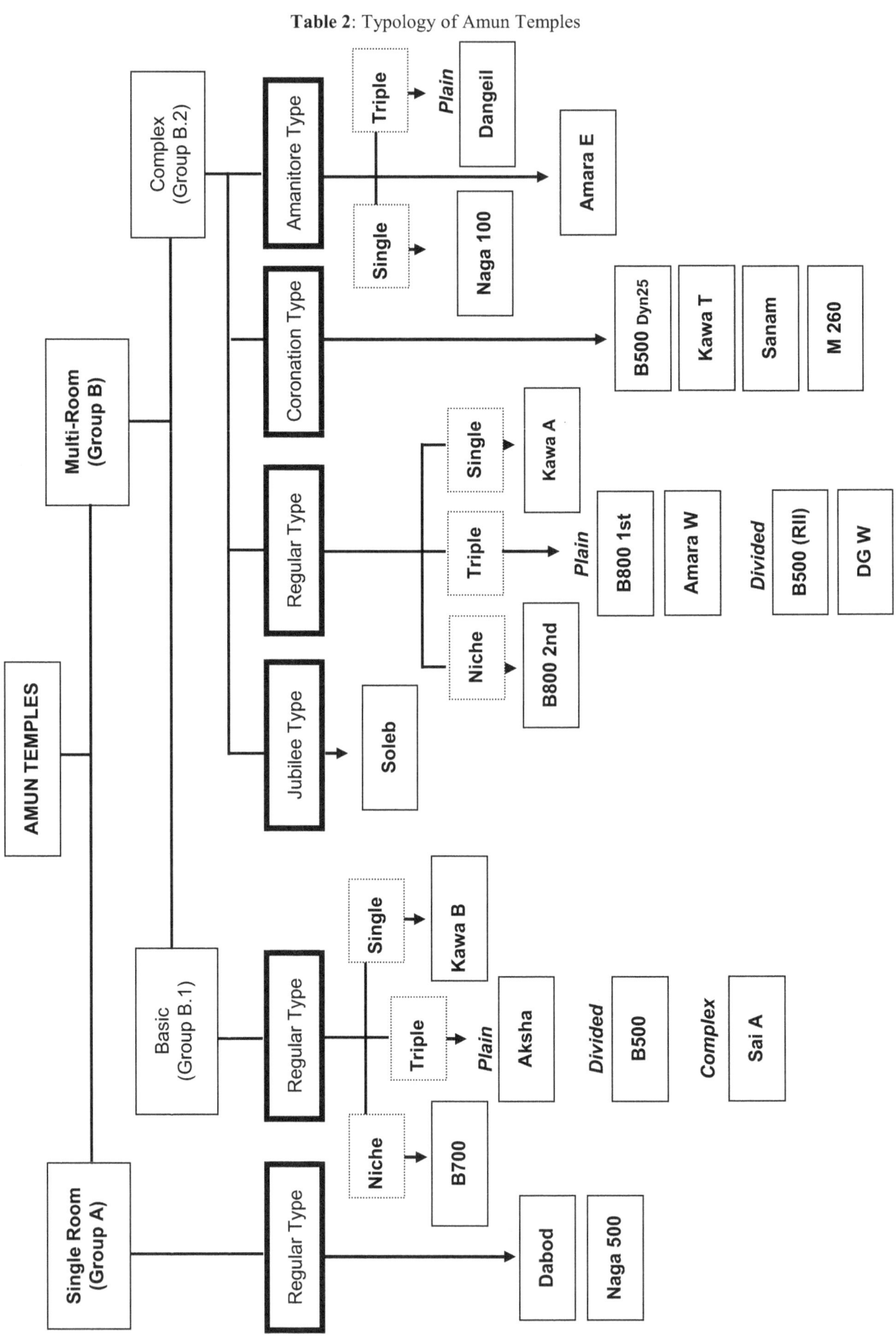

Table 3: Additional Typological Exercise

AMUN TEMPLES

Single Room (Group A)
- **Regular Type** → Dabod, Naga 500

Multi-Room (Group B)

Basic (Group B.1)
- **Regular Type**
  - Niche → B700
  - Triple:
    - *Plain*: Aksha, Awlib
    - *Divided*: B500, Amada, Soniyat
    - *Complex*: Sai A
  - Single → Kawa B

Complex (Group B.2)
- **Jubilee Type** → Soleb
- **Regular Type**
  - Niche → B800 2nd
  - Triple:
    - *Plain*: B800 1st, Amara W
    - *Divided*: B500 (RII), DG W
  - Single → Kawa A
- **Coronation Type** → B500 Dyn25, Kawa T, Sanam, M 260, Tabo
- **Amanitore Type**
  - Single → Naga 100, WBN 300
  - Triple:
    - *Plain*: Dangeil
    - Amara E

CHAPTER 5. SOME REMAINING ISSUES

UNRESOLVED ISSUES AT PNUBS

The Coronation Temple of Pnubs
The recent identification of Doukki Gel with ancient Pnubs suggests that a coronation temple—one of the stops in the coronation journey itinerary—was located on site. The question that must now be posed is whether the architectural remains of the Doukki Gel temples fit the coronation temple type. Although the architectural plan of the West Temple and its later annexes is rather well preserved, the same cannot be said of the East Temple. Yet, amongst these ruins, is there evidence of a dais room at Doukki Gel?

At first glance, it is obvious that the architectural layout of the Twenty-fifth Dynasty West Temple does not fit with that preferred by Taharqo for his coronation temples. As we are dealing with a refurbished New Kingdom temple and not an original Twenty-fifth Dynasty construction, this observation does not constitute a problem. Indeed, it is important to point out that, as has been clearly demonstrated with Gebel Barkal B500 and Meroe M260, not all coronation temples followed an identical architectural layout, but they all included a dais room.

Therefore, comparisons must be sought not with a Taharqo construction, but with a New Kingdom temple refurbished and turned into a coronation temple during the Twenty-fifth Dynasty: the Great Temple of Amun at Gebel Barkal, B500. Immediately, certain parallels are noted between both temples. Ahmed (2004: 212) and Bonnet (1999: 72; 2000: 1103ff) have already mentioned similarities between the small western chapel of Doukki Gel's West Temple (actually erected during the reign of Amenhotep IV/Akhenaten) and the Ramesside chapel at B500.

Another similarity can be found between Piankhy's "throne room" at B500 and the small room located east of the triple sanctuary at Doukki Gel's West Temple. Although the Twenty-fifth Dynasty plan of the edifice shows this room empty, in its Napatan phase it contained four columns, and later, in its Meroitic phase, an altar and a platform. Could this be the dais room of the Temple of Pnubs? Could it be the Twenty-fifth Dynasty addition to a New Kingdom temple, transforming it into a coronation temple?

Although it may be very tempting to suggest it, the author believes that this small room must be viewed in its context, together with the other annexes built during this period. When looking at the entire layout of the Twenty-fifth Dynasty West temple, the resemblance is not with Gebel Barkal's B500, but with the nearby B800. This observation, already made by Bonnet and Valbelle (2005: 67), therefore shifts the interest to the adjacent East Temple.

The East Temple, with active construction phases dated to the Napatan and Meroitic periods, has suffered the ravages of time more than the West Temple. In both phases, the damage is concentrated in the southern half of the temple, where the sanctuary would have been located, near which the dais room would have been built. The ruins that still stand today bear no resemblance to either a Taharqo coronation temple or a modified temple redesigned as a coronation temple, like B500 or M260. In fact, because of the destruction of the most important half of the building, the East Temple cannot even be classified within the typology; it can only be sorted into the complex multi-room group.

As demonstrated by their current state of preservation, the various temples (either taken separately or as a unit) do not follow the architectural plan of what scholars have for decades referred to as a "coronation temple." It can therefore be suggested that a) the Twenty-fifth Dynasty Temple of Pnubs at Doukki Gel did not fit the known coronation temple architectural pattern and its variants; b) the ruins of temple complex at Doukki Gel are simply not the remains of the actual coronation temple, despite the fact that it is an Amun Temple; c) the coronation temple of Pnubs at Doukki Gel has yet to be discovered. Disregarding the last point and presuming that the coronation temple is not located at Doukki Gel, where else could the coronation temple of Pnubs be?

Tabo or not Tabo?
This question thus brings the temple at Tabo back to the foreground. The architectural plan of the temple of Amun at Tabo is slightly better preserved than that of the Doukki Gel temples. However, it nonetheless underwent extensive remodelling and has suffered damages, alas in the same critical area as the Doukki Gel temples—in the sanctuary area. With the inner chambers of the temple in ruins, the architectural plan is difficult to interpret. Yet, even just at a glance, the temple at Tabo shares more architectural characteristics with Taharqo's coronation temples than any of the Doukki Gel structures. Indeed, the temple at Tabo follows Taharqo's established coronation temple configuration. Tabo and Sanam have the same number of columns in the peristyle (twenty), while Kawa T has only sixteen. Tabo's hypostyle hall has an additional column in each row, making it larger than both Kawa T and Sanam. Despite these minor differences, the public part of all three temples was similar. The ruinous condition of the sanctuary area makes it impossible to determine the room configuration. The presence of columns in one of the corner rooms is reminiscent of the dais room. The temple at Tabo, unlike those of Doukki Gel, can actually be included in the

coronation temple type as has been demonstrated in additional typological exercise.

The question of ancient Pnubs thus surfaces again. Literary evidence gleaned from the numerous coronation stelae makes the temple at Pnubs a coronation temple, but the architectural evidence at Doukki Gel does not entirely support this claim. The important characteristic of the coronation temple, established during the reign of Piankhy, is the dais room. The absence of the dais room at Doukki Gel, which, evidently, is the source of the identification problem, makes it very difficult to consider the Doukki Gel structures as coronation temples. At Tabo, the architectural evidence is much more compelling. In spite of the intense reconstruction, the room configuration remains much closer to the coronation temple plan chosen by Taharqo. Could the temple at Tabo still be equated with the coronation temple of Pnubs, even though Pnubs has been positively identified as Doukki Gel?

The fact that both towns are located in close proximity and that one can be substituted for the other in the calculation of the king's coronation journey should not be forgotten. The author therefore notes the following points: a) Could Tabo be part of what could be called "the Great Pnubs Area," where several small towns have been amalgamated to form a larger centre? b) Could the coronation temple of Pnubs have moved from Doukki Gel to Tabo over the years, being in use at Doukki Gel early during the Napatan period before being moved to Tabo later on?

Although Doukki Gel is now officially equated with the ancient site of Pnubs, the question of the coronation temple of that site remains open. Tabo is still the top contender for the location of the coronation temple of Pnubs if it is not at Doukki Gel, undiscovered and unexcavated.

ARCHITECTURE & CULT PRACTICES

The So-Called Dais Room
The temples at Gebel Barkal, Kawa, Sanam, and Pnubs were the most important temples of the Napatan period, listed in various royal stelae as temples where coronation journey rituals were celebrated. These temples played an important role in the legitimisation of Kushite kingship and their respective architectural plans reveal in each the presence of a dais room. The dais room is the defining characteristic of the coronation temple; yet, this feature is also found in the Great Temple of Amun-Nete at Meroe and in the Amanitore temples at Dangeil and Naga. Although scholars identify M260 as a coronation temple based on its architectural configuration, the site and its temple were never mentioned in the royal stelae as part of the king's coronation journey. Neither are the Amanitore temples considered coronation temples in the Kushite texts written in Egyptian hieroglyphs nor in the minds of modern scholars. Yet, the architectural layout of all these temples includes a dais room, albeit with subtle differences in the case of the Amanitore temples.

As pointed out by Anderson and Ahmed, the dais rooms found in the Amanitore type temples are located north of the main sanctuary and the actual dais is free standing (2006-2007: 31). In the coronation temples, the dais rooms are located south of the main sanctuary and the dais itself abuts a wall (Hakem 1988: 112; 115). In spite of these minor differences—which could be attributed to royal prerogative (Anderson and Ahmed 2006-2007: 32)—the dais room remains a feature of Kushite, not Egyptian free-standing temples in Nubia. This is particularly evident at Gebel Barkal, where the New Kingdom temple built by Egyptian pharaohs was augmented with a dais room during the reign of the first Twenty-fifth Dynasty Kushite king, Piankhy.

The function of this so-called dais room has been fervently discussed over the years. Garstang (1910: 63; 1911: 14) and Kormysheva (1994: 206) associate this dais room with a "throne room," the room where the king would presumably receive his crown during the coronation rites. Török is opposed to this idea because coronation scenes were not depicted in this room, but rather in the one north of the central sanctuary (1997a: 122).

Hakem, Török and Arnold have all noted similarities between the dais room of Kushite temples in Nubia and features of the mortuary temples (royal cult temples) of New Kingdom Thebes. For Hakem, the parallels between the dais room and the "altar court of Re-Horakhty" as well as his interpretation of the Nastasen stela (FHN II: 471-500) suggested that the dais room might be dedicated to solar cult rituals dedicated to Re, Re-Horakhty, or even possibly Amun-Rē (1988: 109ff; see also Hölscher 1941: 15, 22-25, 31, plate 2). Török also proposes that the dais room is dedicated to Amun-Rē, particularly because the walls of this room in Temple T at Kawa were inscribed with a hymn to this god (1997a: 122). Török strengthens his hypothesis with the physical connection between the dais rooms in M260 and the coronation temples, and the transverse rooms found in these temples, but also in Theban mortuary temples. The New Kingdom mortuary temples, notably that of Ramses III at Medinet Habu, possess similar transverse chambers behind the sanctuary and these were dedicated to Amun (Hölscher 1941: 20-21). In Török's opinion, these facts combined indicate that the dais room was a chapel to Amun- Rē.

Arnold believes that the dais room had a function similar to that of the Egyptian New Year Festival court, the so-called pure hall, the w^cbt, in Ptolemaic temples (1999: 60). The architectural features of the w^cbt–which include a dais with steps—originate from the solar courts New Kingdom mortuary temple of Thebes (1999: 276). Inscriptions in Ptolemaic temples describe the rituals of the New Year Festival, during which the cult statue of the deity was brought to rest under the throne canopy supported by two columns found in this room (Finnestad 1997: 221-223; LÄ IV: 467-470). Török, commenting on kingship, mentions that, in New Kingdom Egypt, the New Year Festival also played an important role in the dogma of kingship. The anniversary of the king's coronation was celebrated on New Year's Day, even if the king's enthronement had not actually been held on that particular day (1992: 116).

Although the exact function of the dais room has not been determined, what remains interesting is that the dais room is not exclusive to the coronation temple. Should scholars thus revise their definition of the coronation temple? No, the author believes. Not at this point. While the coronation temples share an architectural layout that includes a dais room, it is the fact that royal stelae list these temples as part of the coronation journey that confirms their function.

Following this statement, an alternate possibility should be proposed: the Amanitore temples and Meroe M260 could actually be *Meroitic* coronation temples. Without the support of Meroitic texts, it is impossible to determine whether the Kushites included sites in the Meroitic south to the coronation journey. However, the author believes this is a possibility as a means to explain the presence of the dais room in temples other than coronation temples.

As it is found in temples not currently associated with the coronation journey and its celebrations, an observation of the dais room's possible cultic function must also be presented. Should Meroitic texts reveal that the Amanitore temples were not coronation temples, then it must be postulated that the activities held within this room—whatever they might have been—were not exclusively related to the coronation ceremony and journey programme. In this case, the author believes the dais room played a secondary—albeit very important—role, separate from the temple's principal function. As a result, the ceremonies performed in the coronation temple dais room need not be exclusive to the coronation journey and its cultic programme; they can also be performed in other temples across the kingdom. Accepting this possibility would explain why the dais room can be found in two types of temples as well as in M260 at Meroe.

Whatever the function of the dais room, what must be noted is that the dais room a) served specific rituals that the New Kingdom Egyptians did not celebrate in their free-standing temples built on Nubian soil—regardless of the fact that the dais room and its rites might have been borrowed from Theban mortuary temples of New Kingdom Egypt; and b) is found in temples deemed highly important to Kushite religion and in the eyes of the ruling royal family during both the Napatan and Meroitic periods.

There is no doubt that Naga and Dangeil were important sites in the Meroitic kingdom and, together with Meroe, the temples with a dais room at these sites were the southern counterpart to the temples at Gebel Barkal, Kawa, Sanam and Pnubs, which were important to the Napatans.

The Ramps and Platform at Naga

Various structures at Naga definitely show that Meroitic multi-room temples dedicated to Amun did not slavishly follow the Egyptian temple plan. In the case of Naga N100, the temple was accessed by at least three ramps, from the front and the sides of the temple. Two additional ramps are postulated further along the sides (Wildung 1998: 184). The actual function of these ramps and the resulting platform is still debated. Certain scholars have associated the platform on which the temple stands with the primordial hill of the Egyptian creation myths, the hill that emerged from Nun and upon which the creator god stood. In addition to being the abode of a deity, the ancient Egyptian temple symbolically represented the cosmos (Baines 1976: 10-11; Cenival 1964: 86ff; Finnestad 1985: 3ff). The reliefs in the temple of Horus at Edfu clearly illustrate how the temple was built at the location where the god had settled on the hill (Finnestad 1985: 42ff). Thus, certain scholars associate the platform at Naga with this primordial hill upon which the temple was erected. In an ancient Egyptian temple, however, the symbolism of the primordial hill is expressed differently: the platform does not exist. Instead, the floor of the temple is gradually raised, being higher in the holy of holies than at the entrance. Unlike the exterior ramps at Naga, the ramps in an Egyptian temple are located inside the temple proper, placed along the central axis, and positioned between courts or rooms. The Egyptian temple, therefore, is not built on a platform.

Others scholars have explained this architectural difference with a more practical hypothesis, suggesting that N100 was elevated on this platform to be protected from the flash floods caused by the heavy spring rains of Central Sudan (Grzymski 2003: 52-53; Wildung: personal communication). While the latter could be possible, it must be noted that the ten other temples at Naga do not appear to possess this particular feature. Why would the Amun temple be the only one to benefit from this particular architectural attribute? Only a few other temples in the Greater Meroe Area were built on platforms, notably at Alem, Meroe (M250), and Musawwarat es-Sufra (Temple IA 100); however, none of these structures has been conclusively identified as an Amun temple (see Chapter 3). Another Amun temple that could have been elevated on a platform is that of Amara East. Certain explorers reported that "the whole temple was raised on a brick foundation elevated and separated" (Hakem 1988: 334). However, because the temple at Amara East has since been lost, this information cannot be verified. Could the answer reside in the geomorphology of the soil and the emplacement of the temple? Can the platform be a structural safeguard to prevent collapse of parts of the temple due to an unstable surface or provide a flat and regular surface on an otherwise rugged terrain? Although questions do not by any means provide an answer to the problem, they nevertheless propose alternative ideas that might be worth exploring.

Single Sanctuary versus Triple Sanctuary
Hakem has raised an interesting point regarding sanctuary configurations but has not addressed it fully. During his study of the coronation temples, he has noted that, with the exception of Barkal B500, none of the coronation temples has a triple sanctuary configuration (what he calls the triple chapel sanctuary) (1988: 137). This interesting issue needs to be addressed because it applies to other Amun temples as well. This fact was illustrated in the typology, where the temples within a type were subdivided according to their sanctuary configuration, without affecting the type itself. After a look at the architectural plans, the triple sanctuary appears to have been the most common sanctuary configuration in New Kingdom temples in Nubia. A quick glance at Table 2 (the typology chart of Chapter 4) shows that the majority of temples with triple sanctuaries were dated to the New Kingdom. The exceptions were at Dangeil and Barkal B800-First; B800 was later modified by Anlamani, who changed the sanctuary configuration to a single sanctuary (Kendall: 2002).

The temples with a single sanctuary were either Napatan or Meroitic. The small Temple A at Kawa, constructed under Tutankhamun (or possibly Amenhotep III) and enlarged by Taharqo, was the one exception. This particular temple was difficult to classify because the plan itself is not very clear. The relationship between the rooms in the sanctuary area could not be ascertained. Very little is left of the New Kingdom temple and it appears to have been very badly integrated into Taharqo's later construction. It could have had a triple sanctuary during the Eighteenth Dynasty, as the side rooms suggest, but this is uncertain.

Why was the single sanctuary favoured over the triple sanctuary in the Napatan and Meroitic Amun temples? Changes in the cult rituals and celebrations are extremely likely. Arnold has already pointed out that the Twenty-fifth Dynasty did change the appearance of the New Kingdom temple to suit specific cultic needs (1999: 60). Certainly, this also can be the case for temples built in their homeland. However, the nature of the change remains undetermined. Perhaps the change had to do with the god Amun himself? Mut and Khonsu lost favour at certain sites in Nubia where Amun was shown accompanied by another goddess. At Kawa, Amun's consort was not Mut (of either Thebes or Napata) but Anukis, Mistress of Kawa.[15]

Yet, can the transformation be more profound than just a change in (or abandonment of) consort and offspring? Various aspects—and very different aspects—of Amun have been hinted at: Amun in his role as Osiris and his link to deified rulers (Zach and Tomandl 2000: 131), or Amun and his warrior aspect possibly expressed at Hamadab (Wolf 2006: 252). Amun was multi-facetted. Amun was Rē, Atum, Horakhty, Geb, and Dedwen; he was the Lion of Kawa and the Bull of Sanam (Kendall: personal communication). The Nubian Amun was different from its Egyptian version and the distinction may very well be present in the architecture of the god's own temples.

This new question, though brought on by a change in architectural spatial configuration, cannot be answered with mere buildings. Textual evidence that gives an insight into Kushite dogma is the only possible way to understand how Amun was worshipped in Nubia during the Napatan and Meroitic periods. A correlation between the architectural plan and epigraphic and/or artistic, the author believes, would provide some of the much-desired answers.

THE QUESTION OF MEROE

Garstang and the Great Temple of Amun
At Meroe, great archaeological questions and issues abound. As Grzymski has pointed out, despite the various research projects undertaken at Meroe, archaeologists and historians still know very little about the third largest Amun temple in Nubia. More excavations are needed to clarify many issues, primarily the architectural layout of the temple and its evolution through time (Grzymski 2003: 5). Recent archaeological excavations have demonstrated that the plan established by Garstang almost a century ago is grossly inaccurate. After one excavation season (2000), the great peristyle court, which so many scholars thought had splayed walls, was actually shown to have stairwells that go up the entrance pylon (Grzymski 2003: 11-13) (see Figure 31). The unusual design of these stairwells, which protrude towards the inside of the court, was the reason for what seemed to be splayed walls. Garstang and later scholars had failed to notice these stairs. Shinnie mentioned "kinks" in the long walls of the first court, but misidentified the structure in his Trench G, along the south wall (Grzymski 2003: 11, 29). Now, the issue of the splayed forecourt is resolved. The discovery of these stairwells point in favour of the term "pylon" when describing the monumental entrance. Hakem had suggested that this term was not applicable because of the lack of staircases, that the word "portal" was more fitting (1988: 154ff).

---

[15] There are some differences between the Egyptian and Nubian consorts, if not always in the iconography, very often in the epithets (Török 1997b: 308, but see also Wolf 1990: 192ff).

The 2004 spring excavation season rectified additional mistakes, this time regarding the architectural plan of the second court. The side exits from the second court were drawn in their proper places and the central purification basin was added to the plan. This feature, which was uncovered by Garstang, does not appear on any of his drawings. This ferricrete basin is located exactly on the temple axis, in line with red brick pillars 83 and 87 (the second pillars from the west, 83 being in the north row of pillars, 87 on the south) (Rocheleau, forthcoming). This very feature is extremely unusual and archaeologists have not noted anything similar elsewhere, except possibly in the Meroitic phase of the East Temple at Doukki Gel. However, at Doukki Gel, the water basin is located in the south-west corner of the first court. Unlike the basin in M260, it is not square but rectangular, and is made of red brick instead of ferricrete sandstone (Ahmed 2004: 208). In neither case has the function of this feature been elucidated, but both are referred to as purification basins. The basin at Doukki Gel appears to have held water (a liquid, in any case) as the bottom is covered with hardened mud.

Considering the numerous and important changes recently made to the architectural plan drawn by Garstang, one wonders about the exactitude of the remaining parts of the temple that have not been re-excavated. The present conclusions drawn from the study of the temples at Meroe may be altered in the near future as the excavations continue. Changes are actually anticipated by the excavators.

The Issue of the Early Napatan Temple
The occupation of the Royal City at Meroe during the Napatan period, when the capital was located at Napata, has been the centre of discussion for decades. Numerous blocks and artefacts inscribed with the cartouches of early Napatan rulers have been found at Meroe, and while the presence of an "early Amun temple" has been hypothesised, its location has not been determined. A few suggestions concerning the possible emplacement for this early temple have been put forward over the years. Area M292-298, which is littered with decorated blocks and where the ruins of a small chapel (M292) were found, was designated as the emplacement of this early temple. Hinkel has objected to the location of the early Amun temple in Area M292-298, noting that there is very little evidence for the presence of a fair-sized temple or a palace with an adjoining shrine (Hinkel and Sievertsen 2002: 121). Scattered loose blocks cannot ascertain the presence of such an important building and the architectural remains in that part of the city are most incoherent (Hinkel and Sievertsen 2002: 35). In light of the information provided in Shinnie and Anderson's Meroe publication (2004), the author agrees with Hinkel and Sievertsen. Evidence of an early Napatan structure is scanty. Actually, it is mostly Meroitic.

Bradley, based on the presence of river pebbles in some sectors of the site, proposed that the early Amun temple was the first construction phase of M260 because the presence of a now-defunct Nile channel would have made Meroe an island (1982). Following this hypothesis, the later court of Amun temple M260 and the temples along the processional avenue would have been built after the drying out of this Nile channel (Török 1997a: 29). This would also explain why the Great Amun Temple now faces the desert instead of the Nile River. However, not every scholar agrees with this Nile channel theory (Török 1997a: 24). Theories concerning flooded wadis on the right bank have also been proposed (Wolf 1996: 42).

Although Bradley's hypothesis explains the unusual orientation of the temple, the hypothesis itself is based on relative levels taken across the site during Shinnie's excavations. Relative levels were converted and compared to absolute a.s.l. levels (above sea level measurements) taken by the current site excavators; Bradley's theory does not hold anymore. The foundations of some buildings located in front of M260, which have been radiocarbon dated to 800 B.C.E., are actually located below Bradley's channel (Grzymski: personal communication). It appears that the river pebbles of Bradley's Nile channel are evidence of a flood, not a dried up river channel. However, the possibility of an early Amun temple being part of the actual temple or located underneath it still remains valid. It should not be discarded, the author believes, even if Bradley's hypothesis does not hold any longer. It is the most likely location for the early temple. As the recent work undertaken in the temple shows (see above, as well as Grzymski 2003: 5-32; Rocheleau: forthcoming), the earlier excavations were performed quickly and the architectural plan was misinterpreted. The latest meticulous clearing of the first two temple courts has answered several unexplained features and, as one of the excavators of the temple, the author expects changes in the architectural layout and its interpretation in the other rooms as well.

Other locations outside the city walls have also been rejected based on the lack of convincing evidence, including the *Keniseh*. Indeed, the Isis temple (M600) has also been suggested as an alternative location for the early Amun temple (Török 1984a: 354ff; Zach and Tomandl 2000: 134). Török has noted certain similarities between M600 and M260, but the matter is open to debate. Without denying the presence of an early Amun temple, Hinkel simply suggests leaving the question open at the moment, until further archaeological or epigraphic evidence can support the presence of such an early Amun temple within the Royal Precinct or elsewhere on site.

Although the present whereabouts of this early Napatan temple are unknown, the author thinks its existence is undeniable. Current investigations at Meroe are concentrated outside the Royal City enclosure, in temple

M260, Palace M750S, and the South Mound (Grzymski: in preparation), and Palace M750S yielded the most interesting materials and results in the spring season of 2004. Foundations are all that remain of this curious building, and several blocks that originated from an earlier, highly decorated building were re-employed in the masonry. A number of these decorated blocks were carved with the heads of royal figures, hands making an offering, a row of headless sculpted uraei, a cavetto cornice fragment with a winged sun disc, as well as legs and kilts of unknown figures. The most notable block appears to originate from a door jamb, on which a short inscription was preserved on one surface, while on another was a winged uraeus wearing the White Crown. The inscription, which is in Egyptian hieroglyphs, reads as follows: *mry m3ʿt nb nṯrw nbw*—"beloved of Maat, lord of all the gods," an epithet that can only refer to Amun (Grzymski: forthcoming).

While searching for foundation deposits in the inner corners of this supposedly Meroitic Palace, the excavators discovered a cache of smashed pottery vessels, bones, and charcoal in one of the chambers. A cursory study of this pottery assemblage revealed that the vessels, with their distinctive *obus* shape, were actually Napatan. Charcoal samples taken from this particular room as well as from a kitchen layer located a few rooms away were sent for analysis. Surprisingly, the C14 results were not the expected Late Napatan date suggested by the vessels, but a very early Napatan date of a. 820-800 B.C.E. (Grzymski: in preparation). Excavators believe that the city was occupied and attained relative importance earlier than expected, and that there *is* an early Amun temple at Meroe. The exact location of this early temple in area M292-298—or anywhere else on site—cannot be ascertained at the moment, but the author favours an earlier phase M260 as the possible location for it.

SUMMARY

While there are a number of questions left unanswered regarding major temples in Nubia, much progress has been made in recent years and new discoveries have pressed scholars to revisit a number of hypotheses. The questions presented in this chapter have benefited from a new look in a different perspective, even if most have not been resolved.

CHAPTER 6. ANALYSIS, INTERPRETATION, AND CONCLUSION

ANALYSIS AND INTERPRETATION

The typological classification scheme based on the formal architectural attributes of the temples demonstrated that the Amun temples could be categorised with relative ease into groups, sub-groups, types and sub-types (see Table 2, p. 73). As expected, two main groups have emerged, the single-room temples (Group A) and the multi-room temples (Group B). Wenig had already identified these two groups in his typology, and Hakem's division—albeit awkward—had hinted at them as well. Because the single-room temple group was rather limited with only two examples, very little information could be extrapolated from the study of their architectural layout. The plan was extremely simple, yet symmetrical and balanced. Hopefully, current and future archaeological excavations as well as the study of epigraphic and artefactual materials will reveal additional single-room temples dedicated to Amun, alone or with a co-resident. Should this be the case, our knowledge of Amun's cult and his cultic relations with other deities within such a restrictive space would surely increase.

The majority of the temples, however, were located in the multi-room temple group, the plan of which follows the Egyptianising axial suite of rooms. This group could be further divided into sub-groups, the basic plan (Group B.1) and the complex plan (Group B.2) temples, a division also noted by Wolf. The basic plan complied with the smallest possible juxtaposition of rooms in such a temple: a public court, a vestibule, and the sanctuary. Only one type of temple existed in this category, the regular temple. Although the word "regular" is not very descriptive, it nonetheless suits the purpose of rendering the image of a very simple and basic tripartite structure. The courts—of which there was only one in each temple, except for Temple A on Sai Island, where the court was completely destroyed—were not all identical: some were hypostyle halls, others peristyle, while some others were columned halls. This was a minor difference that could not be taken into account in the classification scheme considering the limited number of temples in the general corpus. However, the basic regular temple type could be divided into sub-types based on the sanctuary configuration, without affecting the type itself.

Three types of sanctuary arrangements were distinguished during the analysis: the niched sanctuary, single sanctuary, and the triple sanctuary configurations. These architectural patterns have been described in context in Chapter 4, but it must be noted that the temples belonging to the triple sanctuary type were all New Kingdom temples, while those of the niched or single sanctuary variety were Napatan (post-Twenty-Fifth Dynasty) or Meroitic. The triple sanctuary sub-type could actually be divided into three more categories, the plain triple sanctuary, the divided triple sanctuary, and the complex triple sanctuary, which have also been explained earlier.

The divisions and the various categories mentioned for the basic regular type temple have parallels with the complex plan temple types. The complex multi-room temples also followed an axial tripartite plan with rooms *en enfilade*; however, additional courts and rooms were present. Such augmentations to the basic plan had been conceived from the start as a single coherent unit by the architect or were the result of multiple construction phases by one or more rulers. The classification of the complex multi-room temples resulted in four types of temples: the regular temple, the jubilee temple, the coronation temple, and the Amanitore temple.

The regular temple of Group B.2 was the extended and larger version of the regular temple found in Group B.1. Close resemblance between these two types was expected, the major difference being the additional courts and rooms. Just like the basic regular temples, the complex regular temples were divided into sub-types according to their sanctuary configuration. With the exception of Kawa A (single sanctuary type), all the temples of the complex plan group displayed the triple sanctuary configuration. The variations were of the plain triple sanctuary and the divided triple sanctuary. Again, the examples of the triple sanctuary were dated to the New Kingdom.

The temple of Amenhotep III at Soleb was the only temple classified in the jubilee temple type. This temple somewhat followed the divided triple sanctuary of the complex multi-room temple type, yet several features made it different from that type. First, the six rooms of the sanctuary area (divided triple sanctuary) were almost literally a forest of sandstone columns. Second, within the first central chamber, a perambulatory shrine was erected. Third, the sun court was indicative of the renewed interest in the sun cult. These few details alone denoted a significant difference in the function of the cultic spaces within this temple.

The third complex multi-room temple type was the coronation temple, distinguished by a particular spatial configuration that includes the so-called dais room. In Nubia, the prototype for this innovation in Kushite temples was Gebel Barkal B500. The tradition was to be followed by Taharqo who built the temples at Kawa (Temple T) and Sanam with this feature integrated within the architectural plan before the time of construction. As a result, the configuration of the dais room was slightly different. At Meroe, temple M260 combined features of both Piankhy's B500 and Taharqo's temples; the dais room itself was a single rectangular room with eight columns in front of the dais, like at Barkal. However, the single sanctuary and the series of rooms on its north side resembled those of Kawa T and Sanam.

The appearance of the dais room during the reign of King Piankhy can lead to the conclusion that this particular room was absolutely necessary in the legitimisation of the Nubian king on the Egyptian throne. However, because it is also found in temples not currently identified as coronation temples, the function of the dais room is still ambiguous. The author believes it served either a more general purpose or that new temples were added to the coronation journey. In both cases, the reasoning explains why the dais room is found in other types of temples. It also emphasises the importance of the ceremonies and the room in which they take place, within Kushite religion. Although this architecture and now-Kushite ritual might have been adopted from Egypt and held in New Kingdom Theban mortuary temples, the related ceremonies were not celebrated in the free-standing temples of New Kingdom Nubia.

The fourth and final type of complex multi-room temple was the Amanitore temple type. Although three temples appeared in this type, only two could actually be discussed architecturally. The destruction of the temple at Amara East is too extensive and the architectural plan incomplete. Therefore, only N100 and Dangeil are featured in this examination, even if Dangeil is incompletely excavated. Dangeil and Naga share a distinctive architectural plan where two elongated lateral chambers enclose the two central rooms of equal width. No columns were erected in these two central chambers at Naga 100, while there were several at Dangeil. This difference can be explained as purely technical: the temple at Dangeil measured almost twice the size of N100 and, with wider and longer rooms, columns would be needed to support the roof. In the present state of excavations, with or without these columns, the spatial configuration of these rooms is almost identical.

The most interesting feature of the Amanitore temple is that, just like the coronation temples, it follows the basic architectural idea of the linear, axial multi-room temple adopted from the Egyptians but possesses distinguishing characteristics that set it apart from the New Kingdom temple plan. In both cases, each temple type has a distinct spatial configuration, which includes a differently configured dais room. This observation is extremely important because it may eventually help elucidate the function of the dais room (see above) and determine the overall function of the Amanitore temple.

Additionally, the internal structure of the Amun temples at Naga and Dangeil is different enough from New Kingdom and Napatan temples to suggest that the Amanitore type can be regarded as the Meroitic version of the multi-room temple. The current excavations at the Meroitic temple of Amun at el-Hassa, presumably built by a different ruler, may yet reveal an architectural plan different from that of the temples of Amanitore and Natakamani. The publication of the excavation report is highly anticipated because it may offer insight regarding the Meroitic multi-room temple, the Amanitore temple type, the function of dais rooms and their inclusion in certain temple types as well as reign-specific architectural configurations.

The results of the additional typological exercise (see Chapter 4) have demonstrated that certain temples not conclusively identified as Amun temples could also be classified in the typology based on their architectural plan. Although it was extremely tempting to suggest that these newly classified temples could then be declared Amun temples solely based on their internal configuration, such unsupported claims should be avoided. Indeed, the architectural configuration of the Egyptian temple makes it difficult to claim that a later Kushite temple that follows an Egyptianising pattern is absolutely an Amun temple. The source of this problem resides in the fact that Egyptian deities were not associated with a specific temple plan. Nor is the problem made any simpler by the presence of other Egyptian deities in the Kushite pantheon. The author believes that after a study of epigraphic and artistic materials as well artefactual assemblages a number of these postulated Amun temples will turn out to be Amun temples in actuality. The architectural plan and the spatial configuration of a temple are, in the author's opinion, the first step of the identification process of an Amun temple.

CONCLUDING REMARKS

Although the Egyptians did not leave administrative and priestly personnel in Nubia at the fall of the New Kingdom, they left several monuments attesting to their presence, including New Kingdom temples, many of which were dedicated to the god Amun. These temples, whether in ruins or not, were part of the Nubian landscape during the "pre-Napatan dark age" and the emergence of the Kushite dynasty, and therefore cannot totally be ignored as a catalyst for the Egyptianisation of the Napatans. These temples were blueprints of religious structures and maps of cult centres that the Napatans could readily take advantage of to help transform Kush into a centralised state more or less based (whenever convenient) on a once-successful model.

Considering the importance of the New Kingdom temples in Nubia, these same temples were included in the study corpus and this is the major difference between the present typology and all other typologies of Nubian architecture. As has been clearly demonstrated, the Egyptian temples of the New Kingdom erected in Nubia served as prototypes for the later Napatan and Meroitic temples. The basic structure remains the same, the linear and axial development of rooms being more than reminiscent of Egyptian temples. The concept of the monumental temple was directly borrowed from ancient

Egypt. Prior to the Twenty-fifth Dynasty, the local Nubian populations had very little need for monumental architectural constructions, the two unique structures at Kerma—the *Deffufas*—being the only examples of Old Kushite monumental architecture. Yet, at the onset of the Napatan period, they preferred the pyramid over the tumulus for their burials (Arnold 1999: 44), and they adopted the architectural concept of the free-standing temple in which to worship their gods, a number of which were Egyptian. In Egypt, the Kushites commissioned enlargements and alterations of already existing Egyptian temples (Arnold 1999: 44); in Nubia, in addition to refurbishing of New Kingdom temples, they established an architectural programme, erecting new temples where there had been none before. For a people who, except during the Kerma period, did not truly possess a tradition of monumental architecture, this feat is remarkable. Although the concept of the temple was appropriated from their northern neighbours, the Nubians did not merely copy it. The spatial configuration of the most important complex multi-room temples in the Kushite kingdom demonstrates a conscious effort to "Napatanise" and "Meroiticise" ancient Egyptian architectural concepts. The coronation temples of Taharqo and the Amun temples built by Amanitore and Natakamani are ample evidence.

The most important contribution of this typological study to Nubian studies is that is has proven this "Kushitisation" with regard to Amun temples. Because the god worshipped within them was Egyptian, Kushite Amun temples are too often dismissed by scholars as copies of Egyptian temples and very few questions are raised with regard to their architectural plans. The Kushites adapted architectural temple plans to suit their own religious needs, although the function of the new architectural features is not always clear to us. The fact that the Amun temples could be divided into specific types, two of which were actually datable to the Napatan and the Meroitic periods by means of particular architectural features, speaks for itself. The coronation temples attributed to the early Napatan period are distinguished by the presence of the dais room and the particular layout of the auxiliary rooms (with the exception of Gebel Barkal 500, which was not an original Napatan construction). The different architectural layout of Taharqo's coronation temples has been discussed by many scholars over the years; however, architectural studies have not focussed on establishing whether there were other temples that followed specific architectural plans or possessed distinctive features (except perhaps Hinkel's 1988 study of kiosks). These temples follow an architectural plan that developed from an Egyptian model, but are different enough to be classified in their own category. They can certainly be described as Napatan multi-room temples.

The Meroites further exploited their artists and architects' skills by creating a typical and very recognisable Meroitic style in both art and architecture. The tradition of monumental architecture, which was adopted via Egypt, was enriched with Nubian innovations and mixed with Mediterranean influences. Török, quoting Wenig, could not have summarised it better: "Meroitic artists knew how to absorb, adapt and combine foreign elements to create new works of undeniable Meroitic character" (Török 1984a: 351). Indeed, the Meroitic complex multi-room temples also have a spatial configuration that enables their identification. The author believes that the internal structure of the Amanitore type—two small courts enclosed the elongated lateral chambers on their combined long side, one of which was used as a dais room—is different enough from New Kingdom and Napatan temples to suggest that it can be regarded as the Meroitic version of the multi-room temple. New Kingdom and Napatan temples do not possess the two consecutive rooms of same width, nor do they have the elongated lateral chambers that frame these rooms. The majority of earlier temples do not have transverse hypostyle halls. However, unlike the coronation temples, which are known to play an important role in the Kushite coronation rites and the Nubian ideology of kingship, the exact function of the Amanitore type temples has yet to be established. Nonetheless, the presence of the dais room in the Amanitore temple type shows continuity from the Napatan temple tradition, and physically demonstrates the mutability in cult rituals and the adaptability of Kushite religion as a whole. The presence of this dais room within two types of temples suggests that the use of the room was not exclusive to the coronation journey and its programme, but related to additional cultic practices important in Kushite religion and performed in Amun temples at important religious and/or political centres.

The architectural configuration of the New Kingdom temple makes it difficult to claim that any Kushite temple following this pattern was dedicated to Amun. The source of this problem resides in the fact that specific Egyptian deities were not worshipped in particular types of temples. Not only did the Kushites adopt monumental architecture from Egypt, they welcomed Egyptian gods into their own pantheon, thus making the issue even more problematic. Although the Egyptianising temples of Kush were generally the dwellings or celebration places of Egyptian deities, it appears that the cult of Amun had also infiltrated smaller one-room lodgings belonging to the local god Apedemak.

The corpus of Amun temples showed a clear two-fold division based on the spatial configuration of the buildings: single-room temples and multi-room temples. The single-room temple dedicated to Amun has not been completely accepted in Nubiological circles, perhaps because it is part of the religious innovations of the Kushites that differ from Egyptian concepts. Scholars like Wolf, Zach, and Tomandl have gone beyond the Egyptological bias and view the single-room temples of

Amun as evidence for Meroitic religious, cultural, and artistic independence. Indeed, the Meroites, even more than the Napatans, adapted what relevant Egyptian religious concepts and architectural features to suit their own purpose.

The present research contributed to the general discussion of Amun temples and heated debates concerning the single-room temples versus multi-room temples. The research was pushed beyond the mere "Amun temple" category of temples. Instead, it dissected the Amun temples down to their basic architectural components and focussed on the architectural variables encountered within this broad temple category. As was demonstrated, temples cannot simply be ascribed to the "Amun temple category" anymore when referring to multi-room temples; single-room temples can also be dedicated to Amun. This is not only because of the misleading nature of the nomenclature, but also because in the course of this research Amun temples have been divided into categories with specific architectural features. These features, the author believes, are a reflection of specific cult practices and each does not apply to every single temple.

Finally, good research not only answers primary questions; it also raises additional ones. The current typological study suggests that each type probably played a specific function in the cult of Amun. The possibility that these architectural designs—notably the different layout of the sanctuary area—were directly associated with the particular aspect of Amun worshipped within these temples is extremely likely. Amun's worship in Nubia was different from that in Egypt, his ram aspect being intimately associated with Nubia. Yet, Amun was much more than just one ram-headed god. Local Amuns emerged across Nubia, some of whom were present during the New Kingdom. The various local Amuns with their respective paraphernalia, distinctive appearance, and varied titles are evidence of the multi-facetted personality of Amun. Various facets and aspects of Amun and the interpretation of his cult were, the author believes, reflected in the architectural compositions erected in his honour. The numerous types of Amun temples in Nubia that have emerged in the study attest to this fact. Temples did not all serve the same purpose. However, the architecture alone cannot express the specific cultic function of a temple; architectural features must be correlated with epigraphic, artistic, and artefactual evidence to further support the divisions into types and to obtain a better understanding of each temple type and its function.

ABBREVIATIONS

ANM	*Archéologie du Nil Moyen*	*LAAA*	*Liverpool Annals of Archaeology and Anthropology*
BIFAO	*Bulletin de l'Institut français d'archéologie orientale*	*LD*	*Denkmäler aus Ägypten und Äthiopien* (see Lepsius 1849-58).
BSFE	*Bulletin de la Société française d'égyptologie*	*OR*	*Orientalia*
BzS	*Beiträge zur Sudanforschung*	*PAM*	*Polish Archaeology in the Mediterranean*
CRAIBL	*Comptes rendus à l'Académie des inscriptions et belles-lettres*	*PM VII*	*Topographical Bibliography of Ancient Egyptian Hieroglyphic Texts, Reliefs and Paintings, vol. 7. Nubia, the Deserts, and Outside Egypt* (see Porter and Moss 1970).
CRIPEL	*Cahier de recherches de l'Institut de papyrologie et d'égyptologie de Lille*		
DAS	*Der Antike Sudan*	*RAIN*	*Royal Anthropological Institute News*
FHN I, II, III	*Fontes Historiae Nubiorum*, volumes I-III (see Eide *et al.* 1994-1998).	*RdE*	*Revue d'Égyptologie*
		REM	*Répertoire d'épigraphie méroïtique* (see Leclant *et al.* 2000)
GM	*Göttinger Miszellen*		
JAA	*Journal of Anthropological Archaeology*	*SARSN*	*Sudan Archaeological Research Society Newsletter*
JARCE	*Journal of the American Research Center in Egypt*		
		SNR	*Sudan Notes and Records*
JEA	*Journal of Egyptian Archaeology*	*VA*	*Varia Aegyptiaca*
JSSEA	*Journal of the Society for the Study of Egyptian Antiquities*	*ZÄS*	*Zeitschrift für ägyptische Sprache und Altertumskunde*
LÄ	*Lexikon der Ägyptologie* (see Helck, Otto, and Westendorf 1972-1992).		

REFERENCE LIST

ACHIERY, H. el-, P. BARGUET, M. DEWACHTER
1967   *Le temple d'Amada*. Cahier I: Architecture. Cairo, Centre de documentation et d'études sur l'ancienne Égypte

ADAMS, W. Y
1977   *Nubia, corridor to Africa*. London: Allen Lane.
1984   Meroitic architecture. *Meroitica* 7: 255-279.

ADAMS, W.Y. and E.W. ADAMS
1991   *Archaeological typology and practical reality: A dialectical approach to artifact classification and sorting*. Cambridge: Cambridge University Press.

ADDISON, F. and D. DUNHAM
1922   Alem, a Meroitic site. *SNR* 5: 39-46.

AHMED, S.M.
1999   The Napato-Meroitic remains at Kerma. *Sudan & Nubia* 3: 39-46.
2004   A Meroitic temple at the site of Doukki Gel (Kerma): A preliminary report (seasons 96, 97, 97-98 and 98-99). In Kendall (ed.) 2004: 205-213.

AHMED, S.M. and J.R. ANDERSON
2005   Le temple d'Amon à Dangeil (Soudan). *BSFE* 162: 10-27.

ALEXANDER, J.A.
1999   A new hilltop cemetery and temple of the Meroitic and Post-Meroitic period at Qasr Ibrim. *Sudan & Nubia* 3: 47-59.

ALEXANDER, J.A and B. DRISKELL
1985   Qasr Ibrim 1984. *JEA* 71: 12-26.

ANDERSON, J.R. and S. M. AHMED
2006-2007   The 'throne room' and dais in the Amun Temple at Dangeil, Nile State Sudan. *CRIPEL* 26: 29-39.
2006a   Bread moulds and 'throne halls': Recent discoveries in the Amun temple precinct at Dangeil. *Sudan & Nubia* 10: 95-101.
2006b   Painted plaster: A glimpse into the decorative programme used in the Amun temple at Dangeil, Sudan. *JSSEA* 33: 1-15.

ANDERSON, R.D., W.Y. ADAMS, R.C. ALLEN, P.M. GARTKIEWIC, P.G. FRENCH and E. CROWFOOT.
1979   Qasr Ibrim 1978. *JEA* 65: 30-41.

ARNOLD, D.
1971   *Grabung im Asasif 1963-1970*. Mainz am Rhein: Philipp von Zabern.
1987   *Der Pyramidenbezirk des Königs Amenemhet II in Dahschur*. Mainz am Rhein: Philipp von Zabern.
1992   *Die Tempel Ägyptens: Götterwohnungen, Kultstätten, Baudenkmäler*. Zurich: Artemis Verlag.
1999   *Temples of the last pharaohs*. Oxford: Oxford University Press.
2003   *The encyclopaedia of ancient Egyptian architecture*. Trans. S.H. Gardiner and H. Strudwick. Princeton: Princeton University Press.

BADAWY, A.
1954   *A history of Egyptian architecture (from the earliest times to the end of the Old Kingdom)*. Berkeley: University of California Press.
1960   *Architecture in ancient Egypt and the Near East*. Cambridge: M.I.T. Press.
1966   *A history of Egyptian architecture (the First Intermediate Period, the Middle Kingdom and the Second Intermediate Period)*. Berkeley: University of California Press.
1968   *A history of Egyptian architecture (from the Eighteenth Dynasty to the end of the Twentieth Dynasty)*. Berkeley: University of California Press.

BAINES, J.
1976   Temple symbolism. *RAIN* 15: 10-15.

BAINES, J and J. MÁLEK
1980   *Atlas of ancient Egypt*. Oxford: Phaidon.

BARGUET, P. and M. DEWACHTER.
1967   *Le temple d'Amada*. Cahier II: Description archéologique et planches. Cairo: Centre de documentation et d'études sur l'ancienne Égypte.

BARGUET, P., A. ABDEL HAMID YOUSSEF, and M. DEWACHTER.
1967   *Le temple d'Amada*. Cahier III: Textes. Cairo: Centre de documentation et d'études sur l'ancienne Égypte.

BELL, L.
1997   The New Kingdom 'divine' temple: the example of Luxor. In Shafer (ed.) 1997: 127-184.

BERGER, C., G. CLÈRE, and N. GRIMAL (eds)
1994   *Hommages à Jean Leclant, volume 2: Nubie, Soudan, Éthiopie*. Cairo: IFAO.

BLACKMAN, A.M.
1937   Preliminary report on the excavations at Sesebi, Northern Province, Anglo-Egyptian Sudan 1936-37. *JEA* 23: 145-151.

BONNET, C.
1999   Kerma: rapport préliminaire sur les campagnes de 1997-1998 et 1998-1999. *Genava* 47: 55-76.
2000   *Édifices et rites funéraires à Kerma*. Paris: Éditions Errance.
2001   Kerma: rapport préliminaire sur les campagnes de 1999-2000 et 2000-2001. *Genava* 49: 197-220.
2002   The Archaeological Mission of the University of Geneva to Kerma (Sudan): Final report following the 1998-1999 excavation season. *Kush* XVIII: 35-44.

BONNET, C. (ed.)
1992   *Études nubiennes: actes du VIIe congrès international d'études nubiennes, 3-8 septembre 1990*. Genève: Compotronic.

BONNET, C. and D. VALBELLE
1980   Un prêtre d'Amon de Pnoubs enterré à Kerma. *BIFAO* 80: 3-12.
2000   Les sanctuaires de Kerma du Nouvel Empire à l'époque méroïtique. *CRAIBL* (juillet-octobre): 1099-1120.
2004   Kerma, Dokki Gel. In Welsby and Anderson (eds) 2004: 109-113.
2005   *Des pharaons venus d'Afrique: la cachette de Kerma*. Paris: Citadelles & Mazenod.

BORCOWSKI, Z.
2003   The work of the Gdańsk Archaeological Museum Expedition in the Sudan. *Sudan & Nubia* 7: 81-84.

BRADLEY, R.
1982   Varia from the city of Meroe. *Meroitica* 6: 163-170.
1984a Wall paintings from Meroe townsite. *Meroitica* 7: 421-423.
1984b. Comments on Meroitic architecture. *Meroitica* 7: 280-286.
2003   Painted plaster murals from Meroe townsite. *Sudan & Nubia* 7: 66-70.

BRUGSCH, H.K.
1879   *Dictionnaire géographique de l'ancienne Égypte: contenant par ordre alphabétique la nomenclature comparée des noms propres géographiques qui se rencontrent sur les monuments et dans les papyrus, notamment les noms des préfectures et de leurs chefs-lieux, des temples et sanctuaires, des villes, bourghs et nécropoles, des mers, du Nil et de*

ses embouchures, des lacs, marais, canaux, bassins et ports, des vallées, grottes, montagnes, des îles et îlots, etc. Leipzig: Hinrichs.

CAILLIAUD, F.
1826 *Voyage à Méroé, au fleuve Blanc, au-delà de Fâzoql dans le midi du royaume de Sennâr, à Syouah et dans cinq autres oasis; fait dans les années 1819, 1820, 1821 et 1822.* Paris.

CAMINOS, R.
1968 *The shrines and rock-inscriptions of Ibrim.* Archaeological Survey of Egypt, 32nd memoir. London: Egypt Exploration Society.

CANEVA, I. and A. ROCCATI (eds)
2006 *Acta Nubica: proceedings of the Xth International Conference of the Society of Nubian Studies, September 9-14, 2002.* Rome: Instituto Poligraphico e Zecca dello Stato Spa.

CENIVAL, J.-L. de.
1964 *Living architecture: Egyptian.* London: Oldbourne.

CLÈRE, J.J.
1977 Sur l'existence d'un temple du Nouvel Empire à Dêbôd en Basse-Nubie. In Endesfelder 1977: 107-113.

CROWFOOT, J.W.
1911 *The island of Meroe.* Archaeological Survey of Egypt, 19th memoir. London: Keagan Paul.

CURL, J.S.
1999 *Dictionary of architecture.* Oxford: Oxford University Press.

DAVIES, V. (ed.)
1991 *Egypt and Africa: Nubia from prehistory to Islam.* London: British Museum Press.

DEWACHTER, M.
1987 Le grand coude du Nil à Amada et le toponyme $t3\ k^c(t)$. *RdE* 38: 190-193.

DRISKELL, B., N.K. ADAMS, and P. FRENCH
1989 Newly discovered temple at Qasr Ibrim: A preliminary report. *ANM* 3: 11-34.

DUNHAM, D.
1970 *The temples of Barkal.* Boston: Museum of Fine Arts.

EDWARDS, D.N.
1989 *Archaeology and settlement in Upper Nubia in the 1st millennium A.D.* Cambridge Monographs in African Archaeology 36, B.A.R. International Series 537. Oxford: Archaeopress.

EDWARDS, D.N. and Y.M. El-AMIN
2000 Archaeological survey in the Fifth Cataract region. *Sudan & Nubia* 4: 44-50.

EIDE, T., T. HÄGG, R.H. PIERCE, and L. TÖRÖK
1994 *Fontes historiae Nubiorum: Textual sources for the history of the Middle Nile region between the eighth century B.C. and the sixth century A.D.* Vol. I: from the eighth to the mid-fifth century B.C. Bergen: John Grieg.
1996 *Fontes historiae Nubiorum: textual sources for the history of the Middle Nile region between the eighth century B.C. and the sixth century A.D.* Vol. II: from the mid-fifth to the first century B.C. Bergen: John Grieg.
1998 *Fontes historiae Nubiorum: textual sources for the history of the Middle Nile region between the eighth century B.C. and the sixth century A.D.* Vol. III: from the first to the sixth century A.D. Bergen: John Grieg.

ENDESFELDER, E. (ed.)
1977 *Ägypten und Kusch.* Berlin, Akademie-Verlag.

FAIRMAN, H.W.
1938 Preliminary report on the excavations at Sesebi (Sudla) and 'Amarah West, Anglo-Egyptian Sudan, 1937-8. *JEA* 24: 151-156.
1939 Preliminary report on the excavations at 'Amarah West, Anglo-Egyptian Sudan, 1938-39. *JEA* 25: 139-144.

FINNESTAD, R.B.
1985 *Image of the world and symbol of the creator.* Wiesbaden: Otto Harrassowitz.
1997 Temples of the Ptolemaic and Roman periods: Ancient traditions in new contexts. In Shafer (ed.) 1997: 185-237.

GARSTANG, J.
1910 Preliminary note on an expedition to Meroë in Ethiopia. *LAAA* III: 57-70.
1911 *Meroë, city of the Ethiopians.* Oxford: Clarendon Press.
1912 Second interim report on the excavations at Meroë in Ethiopia. *LAAA* IV: 45-65.
1916 Fifth interim report on the excavations at Meroë in Ethiopia. *LAAA* VII: 1-24.

GAU, F.C.
1822-27 *Antiquités de la Nubie: monuments inédits des bords du Nil, situés entre la première et la seconde cataracte, dessinés et mesurés en 1819.* Paris: Firmin Didot.

GAUTHIER, H.
1911 *Le temple de Kalabchah*. Cairo: IFAO.
1913-26 *Le temple d'Amada*. Cairo: IFAO.

GEUS, F. and F. THILL (eds)
1985 *Mélanges offerts à Jean Vercoutter*. Paris: CNRS-Éditions Recherche sur les civilisations.

GOHANY, J.
1998 *Guide to the Nubian monuments on Lake Nasser*. Cairo: American University in Cairo Press.

GRIFFITH, F. Ll.
1911 *Meroitic inscriptions, part I: Soba to Dangel*. Archaeological Survey of Egypt, 19th Memoir. London: Keagan Paul.
1922 Oxford excavations in Nubia. *LAAA* 9: 67-124.
1930 Four granite stands at Philae. *BIFAO* 30 (1930): 127-130.
1932 Notes: Excavations at Kawa. *SNR* 14: 87-89.

GRIMAL, N., A. KAMEL, and C. MAY-SHEIKHOLESLAMI (eds)
2003 *Hommages à Fayza Haikal*. Cairo, IFAO.

GRZYMSKI, K.A.
2003 *Meroe reports I*. Mississauga: Benben Publications.

GRZYMSKI, K.A. and I. GRZYMSKA
Forthcoming *Meroe reports II*. Mississauga: Benben Publications.

GUERMEUR, I.
2005 *Les cultes d'Amon hors de Thèbes: recherches de géographie religieuse*. Turnhout: Brepols.

HAKEM, A. M. A.
1988 *Meroitic architecture: A background of an African civilization*. Khartoum: Khartoum University Press.

HEIN, I.
1991 *Die ramessidische Bautätigkeit in Nubien*. Wiesbaden: Otto Harrassowitz.

HEITZMANN, R.
1976 *The temples of Kush: An examination of form and idea*. M.A. Thesis. Calgary: University of Calgary.

HELCK, W., E. OTTO, and W. WESTENDORF (eds)
1972-1992 *Lexikon der Ägyptologie*. Wiesbaden: Otto Harrassowitz.

HINKEL, F.W.
1985 Alim–El Hosh–Shaw El Ahmar. In Geus and Thill (eds) 1985: 163-180.
1987 Agyptische Elle oder griechischer Modul? *Das Altertum* 33, vol. 3: 150-162.
1988 Säule und Interkolumnium in der meroitischen Architectur: Metrologische Vorstudien zur einer Klassification der Bauwerke. *Meroitica* 10: 231-267.
1991 Proportion and harmony: The process of planning in Meroitic architecture. In Davies (ed.) 1991: 220-221.
1997 Meroitic architecture. In Wildung (ed.) 1997: 391-416.
2001 *The Architectural Map of the Sudan: Der Tempelkomplex Meroe 250*, I.1 – II.1. Berlin: Monumenta Sudanica.

HINKEL, F.W. and U. SIEVERTSEN
2002 *The archaeological map of the Sudan, suppl. IV: Die Royal City von Meroe und die repräsentative Profanearchitecktur in Kusch*. Berlin: Monumenta Sudanica.

HINTZE, F. (ed.)
1959 Preliminary report of the Butana Expedition 1958 made by the Institute for Egyptology of the Humboldt University, Berlin. *Kush* 7: 171–196.
1968 Musawwarat es-Sufra. Vorbericht über die Ausgrabungen des Instituts für Ägyptologie der Humboldt-Universität zu Berlin, 1963 bis 1966 (vierte bis sechste Kampagne), *Wissenschaftliche Zeitschrift der Humboldt-Universität zu Berlin. Gesellschafts- und Sprachwissenschaftliche Reihe, Berlin* 17 (1968): 667-684.

HOFMANN, I.
1981 Der Widder von Soba. *GM* 43: 53-60.

HOFMANN, I. and H. TOMANDL
1986. *Unbekanntes Meroe, BzS* Beiheft I. Wien: Modling.

HOFMANN, I., H. TOMANDL and M. ZACH
1985 Der Tempel F von Naga. *VA* 1: 27-35.

HÖLSCHER, U.
1941 *The excavations of Medinet Habu, vol. III: The mortuary temple of Ramses III, part I*. Chicago: University of Chicago Press.

JACQUET-GORDON, H.
1999 Excavations at Tabo, Northern Province, Sudan. In Welsby 1999: 257-263.

JACQUET-GORDON, H., C. BONNET, and J. JACQUET
1969　　Pnubs and the temple of Tabo on Argo Island. *JEA* 55: 103-111.

KEMP, B.
1989　　*Ancient Egypt: Anatomy of a civilisation*. London/New York: Routledge.

KENDALL, T.
Pre-print　The Gebel Barkal temples 1989-90: A progress report on the work of the Museum of Fine Arts, Boston, Sudan Mission. Paper presented at the Seventh International Conference for Nubia Studies held in Geneva, September 3-8, 1990 *(extended version of 1992a, below)*.
1992a　　A new map of the Gebel Barkal temples. In Bonnet (ed.) 1992, vol. II: 139-145.
2000　　*Archaeological explorations in the Bayuda Desert, 1999-2000 seasons. Preliminary report I, part I: Al-Meragh and the Wadi Muqaddam between Tamtam and Korti*. Khartoum: NCAM, 2000.
2002　　Gebel Barkal, the mythological Nubian origin of Egyptian kingship and the formation of the Napatan state. Unpublished paper presented at the Tenth International Conference for Nubian Studies held in Rome, September 9-14, 2002.

KENDALL, T. (ed.)
2004　　*Nubian studies 1998: Proceedings of the ninth conference of the International Society of Nubian Studies, August 21-26, 1998*. Boston: Department of African-American Studies at Northeastern University.

KIRWAN, L.P.
1936　　Preliminary report of the Oxford University excavations at Kawa 1935-1936. *JEA* 22: 199-211.

KORMYSHEVA, E.
1994　　Le nom d'Amon sur les monuments royaux de Kush: études lexicographiques. In Berger *et al.* (eds) 1994: 251-261.

KORMYSHEVA, E. (ed.)
1993　　*Ancient Egypt and Kush. In memoriam Mikhail A. Korostovtsev*. Moscow: n.d.

KOZLOFF, A.P. and B.M. BRYAN
1992　　*Egypt's dazzling sun: Amenhotep III and his world*. Bloomington: Indiana University Press.

KROEPER, K. and L. KRZYŻANIAK
1998　　Naga Project (Sudan)—Egyptian Museum Berlin: The Amun Temple complex preliminary report, seasons 1 and 2. *ANM* 8: 203-216.

KROEPER, K. and D. WILDUNG
2002　　Naga Project (Sudan)—Egyptian Museum Berlin: Preliminary report 1997-1998, seasons 3 and 4. *ANM* 9: 135-140.

LECLANT, J. (ed.)
1992　　*Sesto Congresso Internazionale di Egittologia: Atti*. Turin.

LECLANT, J., A. HEYLER, C. BERGER, C. CARRIER, and C. RILLY
2000　　*Répertoire d'épigraphie méroïtique: corpus des inscriptions publiées*. Paris: Diffusion de Boccard.

LENOBLE, P. and V. RONDOT
2002　　À la redécouverte d'el-Hassa: temple à Amon, palais royal et ville de l'empire méroïtique. *CRIPEL* 23: 101-11; 164-166.

LEPSIUS, R.K.
1849-58　*Denkmäler aus Ägyptens und Äthiopien*. Geneva: Éditions de Belles-Lettres.
1865　　*Die Altägyptische Elle und Ihre Eintheilung*. Berlin: Königlichen Akademie der Wissenschaften.

LLOYD, A.B.
1970　　The so-called temple of Apis/Hapi at Meroë. *JEA* 56: 196-197.
1976　　*Herodotus Book II. Commentary 1-98*. Leiden: Brill.

MACADAM, M.F.L.
1949　　*The temples of Kawa I: The inscriptions*. Oxford: Oxford University Press.
1955　　*The temples of Kawa II: History and archaeology of the site*. Oxford: Oxford University Press.

MACY ROTH, A.
1993　　Social change in the Fourth Dynasty: the spatial organization of pyramids, tombs, and cemeteries. *JARCE*: 33-56.

MALLINSON, M.D.S.
1996　　*Road archaeology in the Middle Nile*. London: Sudan Archaeological Research Society.

MAYSTRE, C.
1968　　Excavations at Tabo, Argo Island, 1965-1968. *Kush* XV: 193-199.

1969 Les fouilles de Tabo (1965-69). *BSFE* 55: 5-12.
1986 *Tabo I*. Geneva: Georg.

MEEKS, D.
1972 *Le grand texte des donations au temple d'Edfou.* Bibliothèque d'étude 59. Cairo: IFAO.

MILLET, N.B.
1964 The Gebel Adda Archaeological Project, Nubia, 1963-1965. *National Geographic Society Research Reports*: 153-159.
1967 Gebel Adda preliminary report, 1965-66. *JARCE* 6: 53-64.
1968 *Meroitic Nubia.* Ph.D. Thesis. Ann Arbor, Yale University.
1981 Gebel Adda. *Supplément aux Annales du Service des antiquités de l'Égypte 24: actes du IIe symposium international sur la Nubie.* Cairo.
1984 Meroitic religion. *Meroitica* 7: 111-121.

MOHAMMED, A.R.A. and K. HUSSEIN
1999 Two seasons in the Fourth Cataract region: Preliminary reports. *Sudan & Nubia* 3: 60-70.

MOSTAFA, D.M.
1992 Architectural development of New Kingdom temples in Nubia and the Soudan. In Leclant (ed.) 1992: 141-152.

MURRAY, M.A.
1931 *Egyptian temples.* London: S. Low/Marston.

ORLANDO, A.
2003 Remarks on the Meroitic inscription of the Soba ram. *BzS* 8: 85-88.

PANER, H.
1997 Khartoum-Atbara Road Rescue Project: Shendi-Begrawiya Section field report. *Kush* XVII: 137-155.
2003 The Awalib temple complex. *SARSN* Autumn: 3.

PLUMLEY, J.M.
1964 Qasr Ibrim 1963-64. *JEA* 50: 3-5.

PORTER, B. and R. MOSS
1970 *Topographical bibliography of ancient Egyptian hieroglyphic texts, reliefs and paintings, vol. 7: Nubia, the deserts, and outside Egypt.* Oxford: Griffith Institute.

PRIESE, K.-H.
1984a Wad ban Naga 1844. *Forschungen und Berichte* 24: 11-29.
1984b Der Isis Temple von Wad ban Naga. *Meroitica* 7: 348-350.
1984c Orte des mittleren Niltals in der Überlieferung bis zum Ende des christlichen Mittelalters. *Meroitica* 7: 484-497.

REISNER, G.A.
1917 The Barkal temples in 1916 (part I). *JEA* 4: 213-227.
1918 The Barkal temples in 1916 (part II). *JEA* 5: 9-112.
1920 The Barkal temples in 1916 (part III). *JEA* 6: 247-264.
1931 Inscribed monuments from Gebel Barkal. *ZÄS* 66: 76-100.

RICE, P.M.
1987 *Pottery analysis. A sourcebook.* Chicago: University of Chicago Press.

RICKE, H.
1944 *Bemerkungen zur ägyptischen Baukunst des alten Reichs I.* Beiträge zur ägyptischen Bauforschung und Altertumskunde Heft 4. Zürich.

ROCHELEAU, C.
Forthcoming The Amun Temple M260. In Grzymski and Grzymska, forthcoming.

ROEDER, G.
1911-12 *Debod bis Bab Kalabsche.* Cairo: IFAO.

RONDOT, V. and P. LENOBLE
2003 El-Hassa. *OR* 72, fasc. 3: 132.

ROSENVASSER, A.
1964 Preliminary report on the excavations at Aksha by the Franco-Argentine Archaeological Expedition, 1962-1963. *Kush* 12: 96-101.

SAUNERON, S. and J. YOYOTTE
1952 La campagne nubienne de Psammétique II et sa signification historique. *BIFAO* 50: 157-207.

SCHIFF-GIORGINI, M.
1958 Soleb. *Kush* 6: 82-98
1959 Soleb, campagna 1958-9. *Kush* 7: 154-170.
1961 Soleb, campagna 1959-60. *Kush* 9: 182-197.
1962 Soleb, campagna 1960-61. *Kush* 10: 152-169.

SCHIFF-GIORGINI, M., C. ROBICHON, J. LECLANT, and N. BEAUX.
1998 *Soleb V: le temple: bas-reliefs et inscriptions.* Cairo: IFAO.

2002 *Soleb III: le temple: description.* Cairo: IFAO.
2003 *Soleb IV: le temple: plans et photographies.* Cairo: IFAO.

SETHE, K.
1964 *Dodekaschoinos das Zwölfmeilenland an der Grenze von Aegypten un Nubien.* Hildesheim: Georg Olms Verlagsbuchhandlung.

SHAFER, B.E. (ed.)
1997 *Temples of ancient Egypt.* Ithaca: Cornell University Press.

SHINNIE, P.L.
1967 *Meroe.* New York/Washington: Praeger.
1984 Excavations at Meroe 1974-1976. *Meroitica* 7: 498-504.

SHINNIE, P.L. and J.R. ANDERSON (*eds*)
2004 *The capital of Kush 2: Meroë excavations 1973-1984. Meroitica 20.* Wiesbaden: Harrassowitz Verlag.

SHINNIE, P.L. and R. BRADLEY.
1980 *The capital of Kush: Meroitica 4.* Berlin: Akademie Verlag.

SPENCER, P.
1996 *Amara West I. The architectural report.* London: Egypt Exploration Society.

ST-JOHN, M. (ed.)
2001 *The ancient Egyptian cubit and its subdivision—Die Altägyptische Elle und Ihre Eintheilung.* Trans. J. Degreef. London: Museum Bookshop Publication.

SULLIVAN, L.H.
1896 The tall office building artistically considered. *Lippincotfs* 57: 403-409.

TAYEB, M. el-
1998 Fourth Cataract Archaeological Survey Project, Kareima—Abu Hamed Section. Comments on the ceramic assemblage of the first season (1996). *Sudan & Nubia* 2: 35-41.

TÖRÖK, L.
1984a Meroitic architecture: Contributions to problems of chronology and style. *Meroitica* 7: 351-366.
1987 *The royal crowns of Kush: A study in Middle Nile Valley regalia and iconography in the 1st millennia B.C. and A.D.* Oxford: Cambridge Monographs in African Archaeology 18. BAR International Series 338.
1992 Ambulatory kingship and settlement history. In Bonnet (ed.) 1992: 111-126.
1997a *Meroe city, an ancient African capita: John Garstang's excavations in the Sudan.* London: Egypt Exploration Society.
1997b *The kingdom of Kush: Handbook of the Napatan-Meroitic civilization.* New York: Brill.

TSINOYEVA, Y.
1993 Some problems of the historical evolution of Nubian cult architecture. In Kormysheva (ed.) *Ancient Egypt and Kush*: 393-419.

VALBELLE, D.
2003 L'Amon de Pnoubs. *RdE* 54: 191-211.

VALBELLE, D. and C. BONNET
2003 Amon-Rê à Kerma. In Grimal *et al.* (eds) 2003: 289-304.

VERCOUTTER, J.
1956 New Egyptian text from the Sudan. *Kush* IV: 66-82.
1958 Excavations at Sai 1955-57. *Kush* VI: 144-68.
1962a Preliminary report of the excavations at Aksha by the Franco-Argentine Archaeological Expedition, 1961. *Kush* 10:109-117.
1962b Un palais des 'candaces' contemporain d'Auguste. Fouilles à Wad-ban-Naga 1958-1960. *Syria* 39: 263-299.
1963 Excavations at Aksha, September 1961-January 1962. *Kush* 11: 131-140.
1973 La XVIIIe dynastie à Saï et en Haute-Nubie. *CRIPEL* I : 9-38.
1974 États des recherches à Sai. *BSFE* 70-71: 20-36.

WEIGALL, A.E.P.
1907 *A report on the antiquities of Lower Nubia (the First Cataract to the Sudan frontier) and their condition in 1906-07.* Oxford: University Press.

WELSBY, D.
1983 Excavations at Soba – fifth and final report. *Nyame Akuma* 22: 30-33.
1984 Preliminary report on the excavations at Soba East in 1983-84. *Nyame Akuma* 23-25: 35-36.
1996 *The kingdom of Kush: The Napatan and Meroitic empires.* London: British Museum.
1998 *Soba II.* London: British Museum Press.
2003 *Survey above the Fourth Nile cataract.* Sudan Archaeological Research Society Publication 10. BAR International Series 1110. Oxford: Archaeopress.

WELSBY, D. (ed.)
1999   *British Museum Occasional Paper no. 131: Proceedings of the 8th International Conference for Meroitic Studies.* London: British Museum Press.

WELSBY, D. and J. R. ANDERSON (eds)
2004   *Sudan, ancient treasures: An exhibition of recent discoveries from the Sudan National Museum.* London: British Museum Press.

WELSBY, D and C.M. DANIELS
1991   *Soba.* London: British Institute in Eastern Africa.

WENIG, S.
1977   Der meroitische Tempel von Amara. In Endesfelder (ed.), *Ägypten und Kusch*: 459-475.
1984   Gedanken zu einigen Aspekten der kuschitischen Tempelarchitektur. *Meroitica* 7: 381-408.
1999   Ein "neuer" alter Königsname. *Meroitica* 15: 678-684.
2001   Musawwarat es-Sufra: Interpreting the Great Enclosure. *Sudan & Nubia* 5: 71-86.

WILDUNG, D.
1998   Naga Project (Sudan)—Egyptian Museum Berlin: Preliminary report 1995-1996, seasons 1 and 2. *ANM* 8: 183-187.
1999   *Die Stadt in der Steppe.* Berlin: Stiftung Preußischer Kulturbesitz.

WILDUNG, D. (ed.)
1997   *Sudan, kingdoms on the Nile.* Paris/New York: Flammarion.

WOLF, P.
1990   *Die archäologischen Quellen der Taharqozeit im nubischen Niltal.* Ph.D. Thesis. Berlin: Humboldt University.
2002a   Die Ausgrabungen in Hamadab bei Meroe—Erste Kampagne, Frühjahr 2001. *DAS* 13: 92-104.
2002b   Die Ausgrabungen in Hamadab bei Meroe—Zweite Kampagne, Frühjahr 2002. *DAS* 13: 105-111.
2003   Die Bronzestatuette des kuschitischen Gottes Sebiumeker aus dem Tempel von Hamadab. *DAS* 14: 97-107
2006   Temples in the Meroitic south: Aspects of typology, cult and function. In Caneva and Rocatti (eds) 2006: 239-262.

YELLIN, J.W.
1995   Egyptian religion and its ongoing impact on the formation of the Napatan state. *CRIPEL* 17, tome 1: 243-263.

ZACH, M.
1999   Vergöttlichte meroitische Herrscher. *Meroitica* 15: 685-696.

ZACH, M. and H. TOMANDL
2000   Bemerkungen zu den AmunHeiligtümen in Süden des meroitische Reiches. *BzS* 7: 129-151.

ŻURAWSKI, B.
1998   Southern Dongola Reach Survey: Archaeological reconnaissance near Abkor 1997. *PAM* IX: 181-193.
2001   Dongola Reach: The Southern Dongola Reach Survey report on fieldwork in 2000. *PAM* XII: 281-290.
2002   Dongola Reach: The Southern Dongola Reach Survey, 2001. *PAM* XIII: 217-223.
2003   *Survey and excavations between Old Dongola and Ez-Zuma.* Warsaw: ZAS PAN & Wydawnictwo Neriton.

INDEX

Numbers in ***bold italics*** refer to an architectural plan or a map.

Abri-Delgo Reach, 5
  description of, 7, 8
Abu Hamed Reach, 5
  description of, 7, 8
Adikhalamani, 10, 68
Akinidad, 40, 64, 65
  Stela of, 45, 65
Aksha, *9*
  Temple of Amun, Rē, and the deified Ramses II, 15, 59, 67, 69
  plan of, *15*
Alem, *9*
  Meroitic Temple, 50, 66, 67, 78
  plan of, *50*
Al-Meragh, 90
Amada, *9*
  Temple of Rē-Horakhty, 11, 62, 67, 72
  plan of, *11*
Amaniastabarqo, 42
Amanikhabale, 41
Amanikhareqerem, 47
Amani-natki-lebte, 42
Amanirenas
  Stela of, 45, 65
Amanishakheto, 33, 41
Amanislo, 42, 60
Amanitore, 16, 33, 37, 39, 41, 48, 54, 59, 64, 66, 71, 72, 77, 82, 83, 84
Amara East, 5, *9*
  Temple of Amun, 16, 59, 67, 71
  plan of, *16*
Amara West, 5, *9*
  Temple of Amun-Rē, 17, 59, 67, 70
  plan of, *17*
Amenhotep II, 11
Amenhotep III, 19, 26, 60, 70, 79, 82, 90
Amenhotep IV, 20, 63, 76
Amenmose, 17
Amesemi, 60
Aniba, *9*
  postulated Temple of Amun, 12, 62, 67
Anlamani, 35, 36, 42, 62, 79
Apedemak, 3, 65, 84
  temple dedicated to, 64, 68
    Naga, Temple N500, 60, 68
    Umm Soda, postulated temple, 61
Aramatelqo, 42
Arensnuphis, 64, 66
Argo Island, *9*, 61
Arikankharor, 39
Arkhamani, 54
Arnekhamani, 52
Aspelta, 35, 36, 40, 42, 62
Atbara-Khartoum Reach, 5
  description of, 7, 8
Atlanersa, 34
Atum, 63
Awlib, *9*
  postulated Temple of Amun, 46, 65, 67, 72
Bastet, 63
  Temple of Bastet of Tare, 61
Batn el-Haggar, 5
  description of, 7, 8
Bayuda Desert, 5
  description of, 7, 8
Butana, 5, 8
  description of, 7, 8
Contra-Napata. *See* Sanam Abu Dom
criosphinx, 57, 59
Dabod, *9*
  Chapel of Amun of, 10, 59, 67, 68
  plan of, *10*
dais room, 70, 76, 77–78
  Dangeil, Temple of Amun, 37
  Doukki Gel, discussion regarding, 76
  Gebel Barkal, Temple B500, 33
  Kawa, Temple T, 28
  Meroe, Temple M260, 41
  Naga, Temple N100, 54
  Sanam, Temple of Amun Bull of Nubia, 32
  Tabo, Temple of Amun, 25
Dangeil, 3, *9*
  Temple of Amun, 37, 67, 71
  plan of, *37*
Deffufa, 62, 84
Deim el-Qarrai. *See* el-Hassa
Dongola Reach, 5
  description of, 7, 8
Doukki Gel, 3, *9*, 59, 62, 66
  Temple Complex of Amun of Pnubs, 67, 70, 76
    West and East Temples (Meroitic), 24, 76
    plan of, *24*
    West and East Temples (Napatan), 23, 76
    plan of, *23*
    West Temple (New Kingdom), 21, 66
    plan of, *21*
    West Temple and Annexes (Dyn. 25), 22, 76
    plan of, *22*
Duanib, 2, *9*
  Temple I, 51, 66, 67
el-Hassa, 2, 3, *9*
  Temple of Amun of Tabakh, 47, 67
El-Messa. *See* el-Hassa
Geb, 63
Gebel Adda, 5, *9*
  Meroitic temple, 14, 63, 67
  plan of, *14*
Gebel Barkal, *9*, 66

semi-rock cut temple B200, 2
semi-rock cut temple B300, 2
Temple B500, 33, 61, 63, 67, 69, 70, 72, 76
    plan of, *33*
Temple B700, 34, 59, 66, 67, 69
    plan of, *34*
Temple B800-First, 35, 36, 67, 70, 76
    plan of, *35*
Temple B800-Second, 36, 67, 70, 76
    plan of, *36*
Gebel esh-Shems, 63
Gebel Naga. *See* Naga
Gebel Qeili
    rock shrine dedicated to Amun, 2
Gematon. See Kawa
Gem-pa-Aten. See Kawa
Gezira, 5
    description of, *7*, 8
Giblab. *See* el-Hassa
hafir, 61
Hamadab, *9*
    Temple H1000, 64–65, 67
        plan of, *45*
Hapi, 57, 64, 90
Harsiotef, 31
    Annals of, 61, 63
Hassaia. *See* Amada
Hathor, 3, 61, 66
    temple dedicated to
        Gebel Barkal, B200, 2
        Wad ban Naga, WBN300, 48, 65
Horemheb, 33, 63, 69
Horus, 3, 63, 78
Hugeir Gubli, 3, *9*
    postulated Temple of Amun of Tara-on-ensi, 31, 63, 67
    plan, *31*
Irike-Amanote
    Stela of, 71
Isis, 3, 66, 91
    of the Abaton, 10, 68
    temple dedicated to
        Meroe, Isis Temple M600, 43
        Philae, Temple of Isis, 66
        Wad ban Naga, WBN300, 48, 65
Island of Djerar, 66
Island of Meroe. *See* Butana
Kalabsha
    temple of, 62, 66
Karkamani, 42
Kashta, 35, 36, 60
Kawa, *9*, 61, 62
    Temple A, 59, 67, 70
        plan of, *26*
    Temple B, 27, 59, 67, 69
        plan of, *27*
    Temple T, 26, 27, 28, 61, 67, 70, 72
        plan of, *28*
Keniseh. *See* Meroe, Isis Temple M600

Kerma, 61, 66
Kerreri. *See* Hugeir Gubli
Kôm des Bodegas. *See* Doukki Gel
lion (statue)
    Hamadab, Temple H1000, 65
    Soleb, Temple of Amun and Nebmaatrē, 19, 60
    Umm Soda, 61
Lion Temples. *See* Apedemak, temples dedicated to
Lower Nubia, 5
    description of, *7*, 8
Malonaquen, 42
Merenptah, 17
Meroe, *9*
    Isis Temple M600, 43, 64, 67, 80
        plan of, *43*
    Palace M750S, 81
    postulated early Amun Temple (Royal City M292-298), 42, 64, 67, 80–81
        plan of, *42*
    Sun Temple M250, 6, 40, 64, 67
        plan of, *40*
    Temple KC104, 39, 64, 67
        plan of, *39*
    Temple M1000. See Hamadab, H1000
    Temple M260, 41, 64, 65, 67, 70, 76, 79–80
        plan of, *41*
    Temple M720, 44, 64, 67
        plan of, *44*
Meshra el-Hassan. *See* el-Hassa
Miam. *See* Aniba
mud plaster decoration
    Dangeil, 57
    el-Hassa, 57
    Meroe, 57
    Qasr Ibrim, 63
Musawwarat es-Sufra, *9*
    Great Enclosure, 52
        Central Temple. *See* Temple IA 100
    Temple IA 100, 52, 66, 67
        plan of, *52*
Mut, 60, 63
    temple dedicated to. *See* Gebel Barkal B300
Mutmir, *9*
    postulated temple, 38, 63
Mḥrekerem. *See* Amanikhareqerem
Naga, *9*
    Temple N100, 54, 59, 67, 71, 72
        plan of, *54*
    Temple N500, 55, 59, 60, 67, 68
        plan of, *55*
Nalsala, 42
Napata. *See* Gebel Barkal
Nastasen
    Stela of, 61, 63, 71
Natakamani, 16, 33, 37, 41, 48, 51, 54, 59, 66, 71, 72, 83, 84
Nephthys, 66
Osiris, 63, 64
Penimen (*wʿb* priest of Amun of Pnubs), 61

Piankhy, 33, 35, 36, 70, 71, 76, 77, 82, 83
platform (feature). *See* ramp
Pnubs, 72, 76
    coronation temple of, 71, 76–77
    identification of, 61–62
Primis. *See* Qasr Ibrim
Prm
    identification of, 62–63, 66
Psammetichus II, 61
Qasr Ibrim, *9*, 66
    Meroitic Temple, 62–63
    postulated Temple of Amun, 13, 62, 67
ram (statue), 3, 6, 32, 57, 59
    Dangeil, Temple of Amun, 37, 60
    el-Hassa, Temple of Amun of Tabakh, 47, 60
    Gebel Barkal, Temple B500, 33, 59, 60
    Gebel Barkal, Temple B800, 60
    Kawa, Temple T, 28, 59
    Meroe, Temple M260, 41, 59
    Naga, Temple N100, 54, 59
    Soba East, 60
    Soleb, Temple of Amun and Nebmaatrē, 19, 59, 60
    Umm Soda, 60, 61
ramp (feature)
    Alem, Meroitic temple, 50
    Amara East, Temple of Amun, 78
    Meroe, Sun Temple M250, 40, 78
    Musawwarat es-Sufra, Temple IA 100, 78
    Naga, Temple N100, 54, 78–79
Ramses II, 11, 15, 17, 26, 33, 67, 70
Ramses II, 15
Ramses III, 17, 77, 89
Ramses IV, 13, 62
Ramses IX, 17
Ramses VI, 17
Sai Island, *9*
    Temple A, 18, 59–60, 67, 69
        plan of, *18*
Saiyal Sirag. *See* el-Hassa
Sakarage. *See* Mutmir
Sanam Abu Dom, *9*
    Temple of Amun, Bull of Nubia, 32, 59, 60, 61, 67, 70, 72
        plan, *32*
sebakhin, 1, 57
Sebiumeker, 63, 64, 66, 93
Sekhmet, 63
Senkamanisken, 34, 42, 62
Serra West. *See* Aksha
Sesebi, *9*
    Triple Temple of the Theban Triad, 20, 63, 67
        plan of, *20*
Seti I, 11, 17, 20, 63

Shanakdakhete, 55, 60
Shendi Reach. *See* Atbara-Khartoum Reach
Sherkarer, 16, 59
Shu, 63
Siaspiqo, 42
Soba East, 5, *9*, 67
    postulated temple, 56
Soleb, *9*
    Temple of Amun and Nebmaatrē, 19, 67, 70
Soniyat, 3, *9*
    Meroitic temple TRG40, 30, 63, 67, 72
        plan of, *30*
    Napatan temple TRG40, 29, 63, 67, 72
        plan of, *29*
Sudla. *See* Sesebi
Tabo, *9*, 61, 62
    postulated Temple of Amun of Pnubs, 25, 67, 72
        plan of, *25*
Taharqo, 2, 25, 26, 28, 32, 33, 61, 62, 63, 66, 70, 71, 72, 76, 77, 79, 82, 84
Takhompso
    identification of, 66
Talakhamani, 42
Tanwetamani, 33, 62
Tefnut
    temple dedicated to. *See* Gebel Barkal B200
temple. *See* name of archaeological site
Tergis. *See* Soniyat
Teriteqas, 43, 64
Thoth
    temple dedicated to
        Meroe M720, 64
throne room. *See* dais room
Thutmosis III, 11, 18, 21
Thutmosis IV, 11, 21
Tutankhamun, 26, 33, 63, 69, 70, 71, 79
Um Usuda. *See* Umm Soda
Umm Soda, *9*, 67
    postulated temple, 53, 61
Usli
    postulated Temple of Bastet of Tare, 3, 63
Wad ban Naga, *9*
    Temple WBN300, 48, 65, 67, 72
        plan of, *48*
    Temple WBN500, 49, 65, 67
        plan of, *49*
Wadi Awateb. *See* Naga
Wadi e Temied. *See* Duanib
Wadi el-Banat. *See* Duanib
water basin (feature)
    Doukki Gel, Meroitic Temple Complex, 24
    Meroe, Temple M260, 41

www.ingramcontent.com/pod-product-compliance
Lightning Source LLC
Chambersburg PA
CBHW041708290426
44108CB00027B/2899